REINVENT
4.0

PRAISE FOR *REINVENT 4.0*

"We are living in extraordinary times. We have greater possibilities and uncertainties than ever before. Our lifespans are growing longer as the time we spend at each job is getting shorter. We must master the ability to continually reinvent ourselves for today and tomorrow. *REINVENT 4.0* offers a cascade of fascinating chapters to help you anticipate disruption and create new transformations for yourself, your career and your life. Learn from Adeline Tiah's experience and enjoy her many insights as you learn to ride the waves of transformation and thrive."

> **— Ron Kaufman**
> New York Times Bestselling Author of *Uplifting Service*

"Disrupt yourself and reinvent. *REINVENT 4.0* is peppered with stories as well as Adeline's own career journey of how they constantly disrupt themselves and reinvent. Adeline shares that change isn't always about adopting new tactics but discovering new mindsets. Whether you work for a multinational corporation, manage multiple gigs in a career portfolio or start a new venture, this framework is equally relevant. Insightful and fresh perspectives that will get you to rethink about the future."

> **— Elena Chow**
> Founder, ConnectOne

"The future is not what it used to be. In this book, you will learn why it is important to think like an entrepreneur, how to take measured risks, and embrace ambiguity, conflict and diversity. *REINVENT 4.0* will provide you with a much-needed framework to help you create your next growth trajectory. This is a must-read if you want to be future-ready."

> **— Chuang Shin Wee**
> Co-founder and CEO, Pand.ai

"Disruption is everywhere and no one industry is spared, it's just a question of quantum. Hence organisations are transforming and disrupting themselves even and we as individuals are not spared either. *REINVENT 4.0* helps one take a good hard look at ourselves to accept that change is accelerating. It goes deeper and shares the eight keys you need to stay ahead. Each chapter comes with a practical guide and stories to help you think about the future differently, and why you need to act now."

> **— Patsy Quek**
> Executive Director, DBS Bank

"WOW. Like **WOW**. Insightful and inspiring work from Adeline. In my line of work, I see many are grappling with the alarming speed of change and wondering if they can find meaning in their work and thrive. There is a widening gap between human's linear progression and technology's exponential growth. *REINVENT 4.0* framework is powerful and simple ! A much-needed framework for anyone who wishes NOT to be left behind. There is no better time for great innovation and reinvention than now."

> **— Patricia Tan**
> Executive Search, Tech/ Sales & Marketing

"Having reinvented my career after 17 years of corporate life as an actuary and a strategist, starting BestOfMe, a digital coaching start-up, was one of the boldest moves I've taken in my life. It turned out to be the best decision I've made in my career. Like me, if you are looking at what's next, this book is for you. *REINVENT 4.0* offers a simple yet powerful framework to help create your future. An insightful and timely piece of work from Adeline for individuals who wonder what's next and don't know how to get started."

> **— Chiew Ai Chin**
> Founder and CEO, BestOfMe

"*REINVENT 4.0* brings a sparkling perspective for us irrespective of where you are in your career stage. Through her personal experience, Adeline brings a unique perspective for us to renew ourselves through constant reinvention. Purposefully crafted for professionals and all alike, encouraging us to work towards lifelong purpose and employability."
— **Alvin Aloysius Goh**
Executive Director, Singapore Human Resource Institute

"We are now in an era where the speed of disruption is so much faster. What does it mean for us, our career and our values, and how do we stay relevant? Adeline hits the nail on the head by providing such a practical framework of what we can do to thrive in this era. Whether you are at a career crossroad, looking to advance your career or planning a pivot, this book will get you to think about your future differently."
— **Yasmine Khater**
CEO, Sales Story Method

"As someone whose career has been disrupted, and who had to reinvent myself multiple times, I highly recommend this book to anyone who is facing the same situation as me. Adeline's many examples and her helpful framework will make it easier for you to find clarity in your future career direction, and avoid the many years of confusion that I went through. *REINVENT 4.0* is just timely as the future of work is full of uncertainty and many will experience disruptions. You will be equipped with the mindset and traits to be in the driver seat to create the path that is right for you."
— **Eugene Seah**
Mindset Speaker and Abundance Life Coach

"Adeline Tiah's take on the Fourth Industrial Revolution is fascinating and easy to understand. *REINVENT 4.0* is a must-read for those of us who face uncertainties and inflection points in our lives in today's disruptive world and yet, want to flourish, thrive and transform ourselves. This book shows you the mindset shifts you can take to make this happen. You will be missing out on your future of change if you don't pick this book up."

> — **Lim Kim Pong**
> CEO, StrengthsAsia + SoundWave Global Partner

"The pandemic has hastened climate action, geopolitical disorder, consumer shifts and digital transformation by many years. This pace of change is only going to accelerate as we enter into the Fourth Industrial Revolution. This will change the work we do – many jobs will evolve, some will become obsolete and new jobs emerge. To thrive through these inflection points in our lives, we need to think about our future differently. If you are looking to be in the driver seat of your career and life, *REINVENT 4.0* is for you. Each chapter presents a trait that would help you navigate the headwinds ahead."

> — **Charlie Ang**
> Futurist and Keynote Speaker

"This book contains wise and relevant advice derived from Adeline's fascinating career journey. It is a timely reminder for us to keep reinventing ourselves in order to thrive in this ever-changing world we live in. I especially like the second 'N' in her REINVENT framework – 'Networking Skills'. Adeline related this to 'investing in social capital' and illustrated the power of networking so clearly throughout her book."

> — **Dr Candice Goh**
> Author, coach and consultant

REINVENT 4.0

Your Keys to Unlock Success and Thrive in Uncertainty

ADELINE T H TIAH

Candid Creation Publishing

Candid Creation Publishing books are available through most major bookstores in Singapore. For bulk order of our books at special quantity discounts, please email us at enquiry@candidcreation.com.

REINVENT 4.0
Your Keys to Unlock Success and Thrive in Uncertainty

Author:	Adeline T H Tiah
Publisher:	Phoon Kok Hwa
Editor:	Eleanor Yap
Layout:	Geelyn Lim
Cover design:	Ryanne Ng
Published by:	Candid Creation Publishing LLP
	167 Jalan Bukit Merah
	#05-12 Connection One Tower 4
	Singapore 150167
Website:	www.candidcreation.com
Email:	enquiry@candidcreation.com
Facebook:	www.facebook.com/CandidCreationPublishing
ISBN:	978-981-17258-0-7

Name(s): Tiah, Adeline T. H.
Title: Reinvent 4.0 : your keys to unlock success and thrive in uncertainty / Adeline T H Tiah.
Description: Singapore : Candid Creation Publishing, 2022. | Includes bibliography.
Identifier(s): ISBN 978-981-17258-0-7 (paperback)
Subject(s): LCSH: Career development. | Vocational guidance. | Success.
Classification: DDC 650.1--dc23

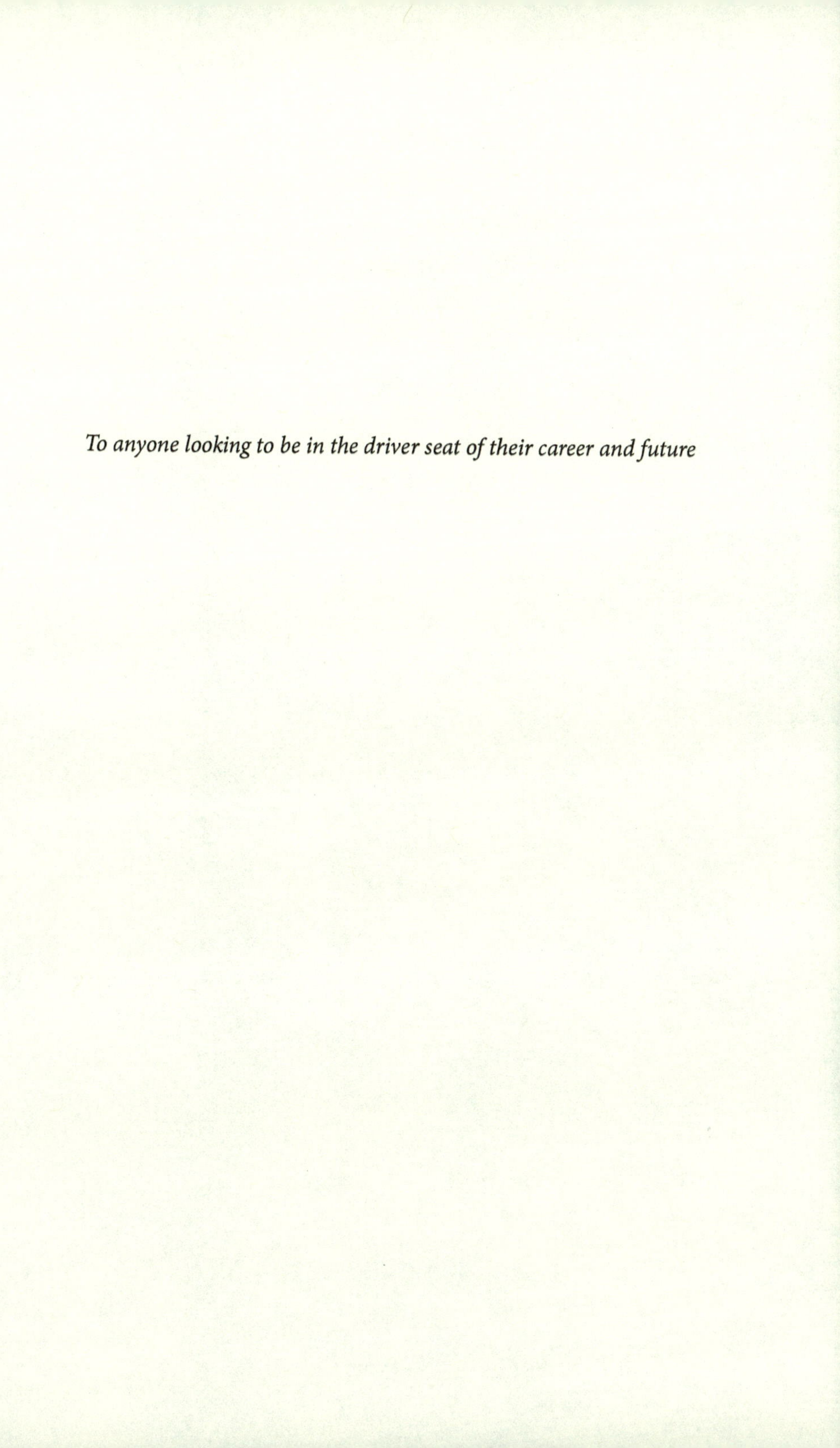

To anyone looking to be in the driver seat of their career and future

CONTENTS

PREFACE

I took a career break in 2017 after working consecutively for more than 18 years. It was a bold decision but one that shaped my thinking about the future of work through very unexpected ways.

I was in my 40s and I wasn't sure if I would still be employable after my break. So it was a decision I made with a big leap of faith.

I have always charted my career path by thinking and planning two steps ahead. At that time, I started mulling what's next and was beginning to feel stuck. For a year, I was oscillating between taking the risk and the opportunity cost of staying where I was.

At that time I was working for a travel agency that was backed by a bank. After two good years where I helped to grow the travel business by 40% year-on-year, I began to feel like a hamster on a wheel. Travel was one of the most disrupted industries with consumers going online to make travel bookings. While this was happening, I was still managing a sales team of 30 agents and more than 60% of sales were coming from roadshows.

With no plans to invest in transformation despite my suggestions, I decided the opportunity cost of overstaying in a non-progressive company was high. I felt I would be rendered irrelevant while the rest of the world progressed.

So I chose to disrupt myself. I had no specific plans. However, a conversation with a mentor changed all that. Over coffee on the first month of my break, my mentor and coach, Lee Han Kiat, who is a retired senior executive and experienced coach asked: "What do you hope to achieve during your break?"

I replied, "No specific plans but I just want to connect with people and learn new skills".

He asked: "What do you want to do after your break then?" I was pensive, then said, "I will still get back to work and continue to lead teams".

He then advised, "Do you know that one of the key skills of leaders is the ability to ask powerful questions? And this is lacking in many leaders. You should consider getting yourself certified as a coach".

That one power question and his advice changed my trajectory.

So I went for the International Coaching Federation's executive coaching accreditation. After completing the course and becoming a freshly minted coach, I began to think how I could practise what I learnt? Then the power of network showed up.

I was volunteering at a social initiative, MentorsHub, as a mentor to undergraduates. There I met a fellow mentor for the first time and by chance he mentioned that a coaching outfit was looking for coaches and he connected me to the hiring manager. I landed a coaching and development role at Ingeus, a career matching provider for statutory board Workforce Singapore.

And I was in for a ride!

Over 15 months, I coached more than 250 professionals, mainly in their 40s to 50s. These professionals were either displaced from work due to technology disruption or stay-home mums and dads wanting to get back to the workforce now that their kids were grown up. Or even caregivers who decided to come back to work after their career break.

It was an eye-opener being on the "ground" and listening to the challenges they faced in getting back to work, such as:

- Younger candidates are preferred; there is unspoken bias of ageism.
- Being away from work for too long and out of touch with the latest work trends and skills.
- Being complacent in a job for too long and feeling loss after the role was disrupted.
- A fixed mindset and reluctance to upskill or a sense of entitlement that the government owes them a job.
- Unethical employers taking advantage of the unemployment gap by offering salaries below the market benchmark.
- People lack the social and professional networks to refer jobs to them (most jobs are hidden).
- People who have unrealistic expectations about their current skill sets and market conditions (that have shifted).

As a coach, my role was to help them overcome their limiting beliefs and equip them with job search tools and knowledge. Wearing my marketing hat, I framed and positioned them for new roles.

The mindshift

The challenges these professionals went through left a deep impression on me. It was frightening as I won't ever want to be in their position. By then I had coached more than 250 professionals and there were sufficient data points to show that mindset is the key to a successful career.

That exposure shifted my own mindset around how I would navigate my career. Being good at what I did was no longer enough. I had to always keep up with in-demand skills. It also reminded me that you are not paid according to how hard you work, you are paid according to how hard you are to replace.

I also began to realise the importance of being able to navigate my career like an entrepreneur – build my network, and suss out opportunities and problems to solve instead of going after job descriptions. I had to learn to take risks. I had to be hungry. I had to be creative. And of course, I had to build skills that create new pathways, potentially building a career portfolio to cushion myself from any disruptions in the future.

This could also give me multiple income streams, keep me intellectually-stimulated and socially-connected when I am eventually ready to exit corporate life. Armed with this new shift, I felt empowered.

I applied my experience as a marketer to position myself for relevant roles and picked up in-demand skills that allowed me to pivot to a role in financial technology or fintech, which is a growing industry sector.

I took proactive steps:

- Built my network in the startup community (to keep abreast on how they are disrupting traditional businesses and learn how they work).
- Levelled up my coaching (to improve the way I led and also create new career pathways).
- Enrolled in an artificial intelligence (AI) course by Massachusetts Institute of Technology (MIT) (to understand the impact of AI on businesses).
- Got myself certified in human-centred design thinking (to augment my marketing role and create a new pathway in consulting).
- Took on strategic side gigs to gain experience in consulting and to solve business problems (and at the same time, strengthen my mental muscles).

- Talked to thought leaders to understand the impact of megatrends on the future of work.
- Joined a community of marketing practitioners from all over the world so I could constantly upskill myself.

I even registered to attend the Alibaba Business School in China, but the trip didn't materialise because of a typhoon.

The list goes on. Lifelong learning should be part of our DNA. It's also important to seek out opportunities to apply them. Most years, I set aside a small percentage of my pay to invest in my professional and personal development. The continuous investment has paid off and has now given me the confidence to choose the pathways and how I work.

Change is no longer constant

Over the years, I have seen many friends get retrenched. The Covid-19 pandemic has accelerated this trend. It has also caused many to reflect on life's priorities and left them wondering what's next.

Just as we thought we were coming out of the pandemic, we are hit with another black swan – the Ukraine war. This has far-reaching ramifications – in the global supply chain, energy prices, rising food prices as well as climate change efforts. And the geopolitical tensions between US and China is creating a lot of uncertainty.

In the short span of four years, we could feel that changes are happening a lot faster. We no longer can rely on the past to predict the future. Change is no longer constant; it is exponential.

If you are thinking of what the future of work looks like, and are highly motivated to succeed in your career and create your best future, this book is for you.

How this book will help you

Experience is the best teacher.

In this book, I share my career journey and the lessons learnt from disruptions that made me rethink my future. I also draw from my experience in coaching to provide insights on what stalled clients' career progression and the paradigm shift you need to thrive in 4.0.

Each chapter will dwell on each point of the framework – **REINVENT.** These are the keys you need to thrive in an uncertain and fast-changing world.

Here's a breakdown:

R – Risk-taking mindset
E – Entrepreneurial thinking
I – Inclusiveness
N – Noticeable
V – Vulnerable
E – Empathy
N – Networking skills
T – Trans-disciplinary learning

In a world characterised by rapid change, we can't predict what the future will look like. As individuals we need to shift away from our old ways of thinking and equip ourselves with the mindset to navigate whatever the changes might be and come out from each inflection point stronger.

I hope that this REINVENT framework will help you rethink the future in a new way and continually build your new trajectory.

The future is here sooner than you think. Are you ready for it?

INTRODUCTION

In the 1960s, many companies on Standard & Poor's (S&P) 500 remain on the list for about 60 years. During those days, the average lifespan was 50 years. Business cycles exceeded one's lifespan so lifelong employment in one organisation was very common. Today, the average lifespan of a company on S&P 500 is only 20 years. And the average life expectancy is 71 years in the world. In Singapore, the total life expectancy is 83.2 years according to the World Health Organization data published in 2020. We now not only have to work longer, but will also experience many disruptions in our career. How can we ride the waves of change and thrive from each inflection point?

In his book, *Antifragile: Things That Gain from Disorder*, author Nassim Nicholas Taleb explains that people can emerge stronger despite randomness, volatility and black swan events around the world. We have always been told that we need to be resilient and bounce back from any setback. Antifragile takes this to the next level. Antifragility goes beyond robustness; it means that something does not merely withstand a shock but actually improves because of it.

At a time of exponential change, we need to bounce back better, otherwise we will end up being at status quo. Fragile items break under stress, antifragile items get better from it.

A good example would be how Singapore always comes out of every crisis stronger because of timely government intervention and far-sighted economic policies. And most recently, the handling of the Covid-19 pandemic has demonstrated her antifragility. While most countries depleted social capital and eroded political trust from how the crisis was managed, Singapore emerged stronger, with a more cushioned economic impact from the pandemic and a stronger social compact.

As individuals, being resilient is no longer enough when everyone else is moving ahead. To be antifragile, we need to constantly reinvent ourselves and adapt to a changing environment. This could mean taking on a new career in a sunrise industry or doing a career switch that is more aligned with your values and purpose, or setting up your business to solve a need.

The paradox of disruptions

The paradox of the exponential change is that we may not be fully aware as changes are seeping into our lives.

The same Internet technology that has caused so many workforce displacements (the decimation of the newspaper, the reduction in retail footfall, to name a few) also offers us more opportunities than ever to do things differently. We can now use our efforts and skills in unprecedented ways that give us a choice in how we want to live our life. For example, you can work from the beach or from a different location.

If you want to build a brand, technology can now help you become internationally-recognised. This could be the perfect opportunity for you to multiply your source of income. You can monetise your experience and skills you have acquired by bringing value to the community or marketplace that you serve. You can also amplify your personal brand and establish yourself as a thought leader and possibly open more doors to advance your career.

One of the thought leaders who has influenced my career shift in the last few years was Charlie Ang. I met him at his workshop on "The Fourth Industrial Revolution and its Impact on Future of Work" in 2019. Charlie is a business futurist, venture investor and innovation evangelist. Deeply passionate about future trends, strategic innovation and disruptive technologies, he is the founding president of The Innovators Institute, an innovation company based in Singapore, and ambassador of SingularityU Singapore, the local chapter of the California-based Singularity University.

During the workshop, he shared insights on the four megatrends that will shape the future and why companies need to be prepared for the disruptions; the same goes for individuals as well. It was an eye-opener to hear how artificial intelligence (AI), Internet of Things (IoT) and blockchain can impact our daily lives.

The global megatrends that will shape the future

So what are global megatrends? They are global, long-term trends that are slow to form but have a major impact once in place. These are the seismic shifts that are likely to affect the future throughout the world over the next 10 to 15 years. These megatrends include:

1. Geopolitical shift
2. Climate change
3. Ageing population
4. Fourth Industrial Revolution

In this book, I will be focusing on two of these global megatrends – the ageing population and the Fourth Industry Revolution, both of which have direct impact on the future of work.

Ageing population and longevity

The world continues to experience an unprecedented growth of an ageing population, driven by increasing levels of life expectancy and decreasing levels of fertility.

The number of older persons in the total population in the world is growing rapidly. Asia will be home to 65% of the global ageing population.

More people are living longer due to successive advancements in health, nutrition, economic and social well-being (FIGURE 1). With better healthcare, people will also age healthily too. What this means is that people will want to work longer either to fund a longer life or to stay mentally stimulated. Work will also give people a sense of purpose and help them stay more connected with their community.

In their book *The 100-Year Life: Living and Working in an Age of Longevity* authors Lynda Gratton and Andrew Scott shares that with people working longer, the idea of a three-stage approach to life – education, followed by work and then retirement – is no longer working. People will need to adopt more of a "multi-stage" approach in their life and embrace lifelong learning.

Country	Life expectancy (both sexes)	Females Life expectancy	Males Life expectancy
Hong Kong	85.29	88.17	82.38
Japan	85.03	88.09	81.91
Macao	84.68	87.62	81.73
Switzerland	84.25	86.02	82.42
Singapore	84.07	86.15	82.06

FIGURE 1. *The top five countries with the highest average life expectancy.*

Singapore is one of the most rapidly ageing societies in the world with a life expectancy of around 83 years. The government has invested significantly in lifelong learning initiatives to boost society's human capital potential as well as to promote personal development and social integration. SkillsFuture, a national programme launched in 2014, provides every Singaporean aged 25 and above with an opening credit of S$500 that they may use to attend approved skills-based courses. The initiative also offers work-study programmes to cultivate a lifelong learning mindset. Organisations are encouraged to send their employees for upskilling to keep up with changes.

Singapore has also set up the National Silver Academy (NSA) to encourage and support seniors in lifelong learning by broadening their learning options. This is to promote a growth mindset and encourage seniors to reinvent themselves even in small ways so they can be meaningfully engaged in the community.

Living longer means we have to work longer to finance a longer lifespan, continue to be socially-connected and mentally-stimulated to reduce the risk of dementia and hence quality of life. Studies have shown that social isolation was associated with about a 50% increased risk of dementia and other serious medical conditions. We will need to shift our mindset of lifelong employment to lifelong employability to do meaningful work and still enjoy our life.

Fourth Industrial Revolution

The First Industrial Revolution used water and steam power to mechanise production.

The Second used electric power to create mass production.

The Third used electronics and information technology to automate production and this has been occurring since the middle of the last century.

Now, a Fourth Industrial Revolution is characterised by a fusion of technologies that is blurring the lines between the physical, digital and biological sphere such as rise of IoT, AI, blockchain and the metaverse. It is a distinct one that is beyond one's imagination: velocity, scope and systems impact. There is no historical precedent for the exponential pace of change.

Today, technology has made possible new products and services that increase the efficiency and pleasure of our personal lives. Ordering a cab, booking a flight, buying a product, making a payment, listening to music, watching a film or playing a game – any of these can now be done remotely. AI is all around us, from self-driving cars and drones to virtual assistants and software that translate or invest such as robo-advisors.

The transition from Third to Fourth Industrial Revolution also signifies the next iteration or phase of the evolution of the Web/Internet from Web 2.0 to Web 3.0. This could potentially be as disruptive and represent as big a paradigm shift as Web 2.0 did. Web 3.0 is built upon the core concepts of decentralisation, openness and greater user utility, putting control and data back into the hands of consumers. To put it simply, Web 1.0 is connecting information to the highway, Web 2.0 is connecting people to the Internet (social media and e-commerce), and Web 3.0 is connecting people, places and things. Sometimes these places can be offline or online even through augmented reality.

This evolution of the Web will be an important shift in the future of how we communicate, work, shop, socialise and even how we bank.

The confluence of these two megatrends – an ageing population and the Fourth Industrial Revolution as well as the recent black swan events – have accelerated changes that impact the workforce which in turn, our lives. How can we be future-ready and live a meaningful life?

This is the premise of the book.

THE REINVENT FRAMEWORK

In my introduction, I wrote about the rate of change and the global megatrends that will impact our work and life exponentially, and that we may not be aware of it as the change is slowly seeping into our lives.

There is a fable about the boiling frog. The fable describes a frog being slowly boiled alive. The premise is that if a frog is put suddenly into boiling water, it will jump out, but if the frog is put into tepid water which is then brought to a boil slowly, it will not perceive the danger and will be cooked to death. The story is often used as a metaphor for the inability or unwillingness of people to react to or be aware of sinister threats that arise gradually rather than suddenly.

We are in the perfect storm now with the confluence of global megatrends and an increasing geopolitical tension which may escalate into a war like what happened in Ukraine. We can expect headwinds ahead with downstream impact like food security, supply chain disruption and increasing oil prices leading to inflation across the board.

While we cannot control the headwinds, we can equip ourselves with the right tailwinds to help us navigate steadfastly and thrive. We need to embrace the right mindset and skill set to weather the chopping waves so that we emerge stronger. Being resilient is no longer enough in the future. The resilient resists shocks and stays the same (not broken); the antifragile gets better despite the shocks, disorder and uncertainty.

To thrive from each inflection point, you will need to be prepared to disrupt yourself and REINVENT each time. Here's a breakdown on what REINVENT means:

R = Risk-taking mindset

Developing risk-taking habits can advance career growth and better prepare us for challenges we are bound to encounter throughout our professional lives. There's really not many ways around it. The greatest risk is not taking risk at all. But how do you balance the opportunity and risk trade-off?

Much can be at stake and the consequences can be life-changing. That's why it is important that the risks you take are informed and aligned to your aspiration and vision. Just like in a startup, you can adopt a "test and learn" approach to help you discover new pathways and pivot when necessary.

E = Entrepreneurial thinking

An entrepreneurial mindset is a strategic advantage to thrive in a fast-changing world. It recognises that changing circumstances, adversity, and even failures are part and parcel of one's growth journey. What differentiates successful people is the determination and tenacity that they possess in overcoming challenges, setbacks and mistakes. As you manage your career, don't think in terms of job description. Instead find out the emerging trends, opportunities and problems you can help solve.

Developing learning agility will help you evolve and build a range of perspectives. Being entrepreneurial also means constantly seeking new "engines of growth" and to help you navigate your career, and direct your learning to be ready for the next growth trajectory or new opportunities. You will be highly sought after for your intrinsic sense of ambition, motivation and accountability, all of which will drive you to continually improve yourself.

In a Volatile, Uncertain, Complex and Ambiguous (VUCA) world that will continue to drive unrelenting changes across the globe, maintaining status quo is no longer a viable option. Individuals who want to be meaningfully engaged at work, today as well as in the future, will need to embrace an entrepreneurial mindset.

I = Inclusiveness

With people working longer and retiring later, this decade sees the most number of generations working together. This includes the Baby Boomers II (people born from 1955 to 1964, during the post-World War II baby boom), Generation X (born between 1965 and 1980), Gen Y or Millennials (born between 1981 and 1996) and Gen Z (born between 1997 and 2012) (FIGURE 2).

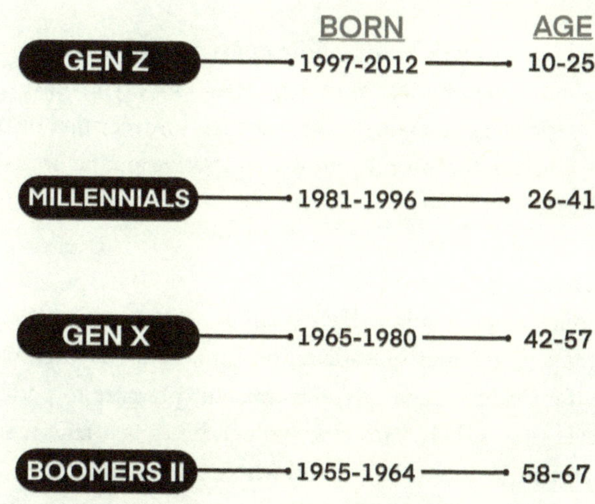

FIGURE 2. *The age band of the different generations.*

What this means is that you will need to embrace and be open to diversity, be inclusive and equip yourself with the skills to manage conflicts, ambiguity (as a different generation has different perspectives and styles of communication) and harness ideas from different perspectives. This translates to having the ability to manage different types of stakeholders. Diversity is a fact, inclusiveness is a choice. This skill will never be replaced by technology and will be more important in the future of work.

N = Noticeable

In a highly connected world where talents can be sourced from anywhere, there is more competition for every job opportunity. Social media has also created a platform to amplify your brand, but it has also created a world of misinformation and fake news. To differentiate yourself and get noticed, you need to manage your own story. Being highly visible and yet consistent is important. Your personal branding strategy stems from who you are, what you stand for, your unique value proposition (your brand positioning – what you want to be known for) and your personality.

Your brand strategy will be the guiding post for your message, content, channels and collaboration with partners. Once you have a social presence, you will have a googleable record so any recruiter or prospect can check you out. So control your own narrative and be noticeable for the right reasons.

V = Vulnerable

Conventionally, being vulnerable is seen as a weakness, particularly in business. When it comes to leadership, vulnerability is often treated as a liability for leaders. Leaders feel a constant pressure to perform at a higher level than others. However, vulnerability is a true measure of courage and authenticity. In a world where people show their best self on a social platform or at work to appear as perfect or even invincible, being authentic makes you more relatable.

Even though it may feel uncomfortable, it portrays you as a real person rather than a robot. When we hear the stories of successful people, we are frequently inspired by the circumstances and obstacles they were able to overcome along their path. Although it may seem paradoxical, showing vulnerability is actually showing strength. Exhibiting such authenticity and speaking truthfully about vulnerabilities is the essence of a growth mindset, because you accept your imperfections and are open to improving yourself. This makes you more human in a future where technology will be a key focus.

E = Empathy

With globalisation, where the world is becoming increasingly interconnected, besides different generations, we will get to work with people from diverse backgrounds. The ability to understand different values, perspectives and cultural nuances will be valuable skills in our career. Empathy will improve our capacity to communicate with others, to be part of a team and to better our leadership skill, which is becoming one of the most important tasks of the 21st century.

Daniel Goleman, author of *Emotional Intelligence: Why It Can Matter More Than IQ* and other researchers have consistently identified empathy as a core component of emotional intelligence and a powerful predictor of success in the workplace. It helps us develop deep levels of rapport and trust with others both at work and in other aspects of our lives. These qualities are also increasingly important to employers as they search for workers who are team players, can demonstrate critical thinking, and have the ability to quickly adapt to new learnings or situations. In the future of work, the ability to build a more collaborative relationship will give you a competitive advantage.

N = Networking skills

Who you know is what you know. Pursue a no-agenda relationship building and be genuinely interested in the person if you want to build meaningful connections. Networking is like building an emotional bank account. Create value for your network, make an emotional bank deposit just like you build an emergency bank account. The person you meet may have no professional relevance to you now. But over time, career and life trajectories change and you will never know when you can influence each other in an unexpected way.

T = Trans-disciplinary learning

The question about being a specialist or generalist is no longer relevant in the future of work. Today's world is more complex than it's ever been, as are the problems that this diverse, connected world creates. Thus, it's never been more important for people to be able to connect the dots between different subjects to come up with comprehensive, creative solutions. In fact, based on the World Economic Forum (WEF) Future of Jobs report in 2020, the number one skill by 2025 is analytical thinking and innovation.

Building different fields of knowledge can give you an information advantage that fuels innovation. For example, marketers will now need to understand technology or build the right tech stack to track marketing effectiveness. Human resource practitioners will need to embrace data analytics to predict staff attrition and understand staff engagement. This enables them to channel their resources to solve the right problems.

In the future of work, having an innate sense of curiosity, the ability to learn and find ways to apply new skills are ever more important.

Why reinventing matters?

In our lifetime, we will continue to experience much volatility and disruptions. As organisations speed up their transformation to protect their business margins and find new growth engines, new jobs will be created and some existing ones will also evolve.

Career success is no longer following a defined, lockstep path. It's about being able to constantly renew and reinvent yourself, taking risks and putting yourself in front of more and evolving opportunities. Uncertainty and disruptions are the new markers of the world we live in today. Careers are taking on new and different shapes, and technology will change our futures in ways that have never been possible before.

So get ready to REINVENT.

1 RISK-TAKING MINDSET

"The biggest risk is not taking any risk … in a world that is changing really quickly, the only strategy that is guaranteed to fail is not taking risks."

– Mark Zuckerberg, CEO and founder, Meta

At 25 years old, I got retrenched as the retail principal whom I worked for, decided to withdraw the distributorship.

When one door closes, two doors open for me.

I was presented with two great career opportunities – a business role at Citibank and a product marketing role at a yet to be launched telco startup. It was a tough decision. One was an unknown startup with the potential to disrupt an industry while the other was an international bank with a global footprint and opportunities for regional roles. The glamour of working for an MNC with a good starting pay was also tempting. Furthermore, it was a hard-earned role as I cleared several rounds of interviews.

With no coaches or career mentors, I relied on books to help me navigate my career. *Horse Sense: The Key to Success is Finding a Horse to Ride* by Al Ries and Jack Trout written by two renowned marketers, offers a decidedly different approach to career management. It was that book that guided my career decision.

Taking a calculated risk

I happened to be reading the book at the time when I was presented with the two opportunities. The central idea of the book is that hard work is not what leads to success. Specifically in one of the chapters titled "The Company Horse", the authors frame the odds of success riding the company horse is 50:1 (relative to others). The principle? The larger the company, the higher the odds; the smaller the company, the lower the odds. Yet the paradox is that most people want to work for big organisations because they perceive that's where the opportunities are.

So coming back to my situation, a big and prestigious company like Citibank is a good place to get my ticket punched. A great brand name on my resume might parlay my experience to get a ride on a better horse next time. To get ahead, you want to be in a role that gives you greater visibility in the organisation and the industry. I had to decide if I wanted to be a small fish in a big pond or a small fish in a small pond (with the potential to grow to a bigger pond). What are the odds of success?

I took a calculated risk. Banking could wait. How often does one get the chance to disrupt an industry and challenge an incumbent? Besides the startup involved a sunrise industry with a very high probability of success. The idea of being a David against the Goliath was exciting for me. Plus I was young and felt I could take the risk. What is the worst that could happen if I didn't make it?

I decided to take up a less glamorous but more exciting job at M1 with a lower pay. That was the role that gave me a career breakthrough.

The ride gave me invaluable experience and exponential growth in my marketing career. I had amazing bosses who believed in me. They put me in roles that I had no experience in. In the nine years there, I held three roles with each role having bigger responsibilities. Over time, I had developed a learning agility. The journey gave me many firsts:

- Launched many firsts in the market that disrupted the telco industry (only to be copied by the incumbent a few months later).
- Managed a S$20-million annual advertising budget that allowed me to flex my creativity and built a strong professional and personal network.
- Launched and implemented a Customer Relationship Management system that brought me to Austria, London and Hong Kong for the evaluation (yes on business-class travel during those days).
- Built great campaigns that won marketing awards and got invited to speak at industry events in Hong Kong, Manila and Bangkok.
- Built my marketing experience across branding, product marketing, loyalty marketing and business analytics.
- Got an attachment in Hong Kong and Sydney to understudy the telco landscape and business strategy.
- Gained valuable leadership lessons from managing team conflicts to leadership mistakes like lack of trust and micromanaging.

And to top it all, I built great friendships (both within the organisation and the industry) along the way and some of them have become my travel buddies.

Taking more risks

My next journey was with a global bank, eventually. This time it was with HSBC. Making the decision to change industry was hard. But I felt I had to give up the comfort of the familiar and put up with the stress of the unfamiliar to stretch myself. At the time, I believed the future of banking is in wealth management.

In an industry steeped in tradition and culture, the psychological safety was low. The first six months was a struggle for me. There were established cliques and circles that were hard to break in. Office politics was common. But I was determined to gain a foothold; if I leave this new industry without giving myself a chance to succeed or fail, it would not do justice for my move. I shouldered on.

Before I knew it, I had spent more than seven years in financial services across two banks and various functions in the wealth management industry and eventually, I was seconded to a travel subsidiary of the bank.

Travel was one of my best rides! A fast-moving consumer industry, the pace was fast. I got to manage the sales, marketing and product functions, flexing my muscles with an expanded role. Travel is a very tough business because it is highly disrupted with very low business margins and high customer expectations. Being part of the bank gave me leverage to negotiate creatively with the airlines, tourism boards and hotels. Sales grew 40% year-on-year. I also enjoyed travel perks when I travelled.

While it was fun and I had great colleagues, overstaying in a sunset organisation meant career suicide in the long term. I stopped getting calls from recruiters because a travel agency is non-progressive. And I wasn't growing on the job. I began to wonder if I should risk quitting without a job or what was the opportunity cost of staying in a company that is sunsetting?

And it so happened when the travel business had a realignment of their business strategy, they offered me a role back at the bank. That was not very exciting. I did my sums. I had sufficient financial runway to take a career break for two years and I did just that.

Opportunity and risk trade-off

How much risk should we take? What is the opportunity trade-off?

If we study the careers of highly successful people, we'll find an enormous amount of mental flexibility. They are able not just to recognise a good opportunity, but to take decisive action to seize the opportunity before it blows away. Sadly, many people are frozen in time. So when do you take a risk?

Changing jobs or switching careers is one of our biggest decisions we have to make. More than just a bigger pay package or bigger role, sometimes the decision may not be so clear-cut. Here's a checklist of when you could possibly have a higher opportunity cost if you don't take the risk:

- **You're not advancing anymore:** If you've hit a ceiling at your job and feel as if you're wasting your potential, it's probably best to start looking for another opportunity to use your talents.
- **You're bored at work:** When your work becomes boring, your performance can suffer because you might not be motivated to work as hard as usual. This means it's time to look for a new direction.
- **Your life is changing:** When your life is in flux or your priorities have changed, these can create a natural inclination to make a change in your career.
- **You have a calling:** Yes, you can pursue a calling and make money at the same time or what drive you have changed. You'll feel dissatisfied in your career until you pivot towards your calling.
- **Your company situation has changed and your role is at risk:** If you can see signs that you are on a sinking ship, it's time to make the move.
- **Your company is in a sunset industry:** This is where the longer you stay, the more irrelevant you will become.
- **Your work is not duly recognised:** When a new management is parachuted in and you are being sidelined.

- **Your mental health is affected:** When the environment is just too toxic and you have done your best to change things around.

When you are not sure about taking the risk, you can start by taking a low-cost probe or something like a test drive. You can start by doing a side hustle and see if you enjoy doing it or if that is what you want to do in the long run.

The risks we take in life should be the most informed decisions we will make, because they can be life-changing. And when you are experiencing fear in taking the risk or pursuing any opportunity, ask yourself why. What are you afraid of exactly? If it's a possibility that you'll experience a short-term setback, such as being rejected or failing, play the long game. Try viewing the experience as if you were a few years older. Then consider the opportunity from the same vantage point. What's the best-case scenario if you seize the opportunity? What would your life look like as a result of the "risk" you take? How do you feel about it? How does this align with your aspirations and longer term goal?

When you play the long game, the decisions you take should align with your vision and the life you want to lead. When you change or see things in new perspectives, big things can be seen as little things and it becomes harder to worry about anything.

Making the decision to take risks

We all go through that, for some of us many times over. Oscillating over the options, weighing if the risk is worth taking. How do we make decisions to take risks? There are three actions I take to make decisions:

1. **Reframe perspectives** – Reframing is about creating a new way to look at the situation. Finding a new lens or perspective to overcome

your limiting beliefs so you can move forward. Some examples of how you can reframe your own narrative:

"I believe I am not smart."
Reframed it becomes ... "Because I do not know enough,
I am curious to find out more."

"I believe I'm not good enough."
Reframed it becomes ... "When I put my mind to it and practise patience and self-compassion, I can learn anything I want and excel."

This reframing exercise is just the tip of the iceberg in learning to recognise and release these habits in a more constructive and productive way. It also lends a new perspective to taking risks and helps you make better decisions.

2.   **Evaluate your options** – List down the options on a piece of paper. Under each option, create two rows – "What's so good about this option?" and "What's not so good about this option?"

3.   **Prioritise what matters now and in the future** – Once you have listed down your reasons, in the four quadrants, you can prioritise them by ranking the reasons based on what matters to you now and in the future.

This is what it would look like as an example:

	Option A – Staying in the current job	Option B – Taking on a different role/career switch
What's so good about this?	**Quadrant 3** • Income stability (4) • Great colleagues • Good staff benefits (5)	**Quadrant 4** • Fresh new challenge (1) • Pursue an interesting and different role (2) • Make new connections, widen perspectives (3)
What's not so good about this?	**Quadrant 1** • Lack of career progression • Exhausted all career growth options • Long hours	**Quadrant 2** • May have to take a pay cut • Steep learning curve • Risk of job security

Based on the above ranking, it becomes very clear that what's important in this case falls under option B – quadrant 4. In quadrant 3 – income stability and good staff benefits are ranked lower. But making a successful career switch in the right company could bring income stability and staff benefits (reframe).

I have used this exercise to help me distil my thinking and aid in my decision-making. Writing them down helps because it is an exercise to bring out what's in your unconscious mind to the conscious state on paper. If you are still not sure? Visualise what's important for you in the long term, what drives you and what are your strengths. Read the last chapter, Create the Future You.

A RISK THAT PAID OFF

Sophia Yeow is an amazing woman who left a high-flying career at a global MNC to chart a new path, one that leverages on her other talent.

Fast forward, two years after she left the corporate treadmill, she entered the MasterChef Singapore Season 2 in 2020 and landed in 13th place. In 2021, she won the Lee Kum Kee Supreme Chef II Champion title.

In 2017 during a coaching session, when I met her, she was mulling at the option of starting her own business but decided to put that on the back-burner and went back to the corporate world instead. But on her bucket list, she listed that she wanted to be entrepreneur. So while working, she roped in a friend with a similar professional profile as her and sat down to brainstorm. After some research, they arrived at running a holistic children's education centre and found that this was a growth area.

They managed to convince the owner of a UK franchise to believe in them. They then re-packaged the programme with a local appeal. This is all while she was still in her day job. In their programme, they invited a speaker to share real-work perspectives which allowed the students to feel engaged. In addition, they taught the children aged three to 12 about the value of money! They installed a little commercial platform in their enrichment centre where the children who worked hard were rewarded with stars that they could redeem for items of their choice.

Being a mother of two, building a side hustle was tough for Sophia. But when there is a will, there is a way. Her business acumen was also put to test. Two years into the business, investors were knocking on her door and this was a validation that she was on the right track. Just as she was planning to expand the business across Asia (and possibly quitting her day job), she met with a near death accident and her business partner's husband had an expatriate opportunity. They decided to sell the lucrative business and take a career break to recharge and recalibrate.

Not too long after, she was head-hunted back to corporate. But the entrepreneur spirit in her was strong and she decided to take the risk once again. It was a risk indeed, as Covid-19 hit just after that. During the pandemic, her friends were going to her for support in their meal plans. Recognising an opportunity, she launched her home-based business and built her own brand – TiaptiapwithSoph – delivering comfort food at accessible prices with cost-effective packaging.

She had hit a sweet spot – doing what she is good at (creating culinary experiences) and leveraging her network and referral to grow her business.

In 2020, she decided to get out of her comfort zone again to try going on MasterChef and the Lee Kum Kee Supreme Chef II.

Sharing her advice on taking risks: "Risks don't have to be reckless. You can take steps to increase the chances of success. For example, I tried it as a side-hustle before I quit my job. I made sure I did something that leveraged on my strengths and be humble to take feedback as they come. If it's positive, it's great affirmation; if it's not too pleasing to the ear, seek to improve and get better!

"Don't be afraid to fail. Doing things that scares you can help you learn to tolerate uncertainty and anxiety. It expands your perspectives and provides you with a chance to sharpen your skills and learn from your mistakes. With practice, you can get better at calculating risk. And as you improve, your chances of success will skyrocket."

SUMMARY

The past can no longer predict the future. Because of this, your ability to take risks and reinvent yourself will help you navigate the headwinds. Be open to pursue interesting experiences as these could open up possibilities that otherwise might have been hidden or inaccessible.

There are millions of reasons not to try something new, especially if it means stepping out of the comfort zone. Excuses such as timing is not right or something more important takes precedence over the action you want to take. When you are stuck, the following checklist can help you move forward:

1. Understanding your long-term vision and aspirations will help you weigh the opportunities and risks so that you can make a more informed decision.
2. If unsure, try a low-cost probe (test and learn) to mitigate any risk.
3. A risk-thinking mindset will possibly open more doors when you:
   - Reframe your perspectives.
   - Cultivate a growth mindset.

When taking risks becomes part of your DNA, your ability to adapt and grow will help you bounce back better from any inflection points ahead.

Take (calculated) risks. Be fearless. Don't worry about the possibility of failing or looking foolish. You are human and everyone knows that already.

2 ENTREPRENEURIAL THINKING

"Society flourishes when people think entrepreneurially."

– Reid Hoffman, co-author of Startup of You: Adapt, Take Risks, Grow Your Network, and Transform Your Career

Working in a startup and hanging out with people in the community has made me more agile and stretched my ability to wear many hats. Transiting from big and traditional organisations to startups has changed my paradigm of work. In big organisations, we tend to follow the corporate policies and direction. However, in a startup, to thrive you have to be a self-starter, be willing to roll up your sleeves, wear many hats at the same time and also put on a consulting hat.

So when I started on this writing journey, I put on my entrepreneurial hat and applied the design thinking framework for the whole journey.

I completed 34,000 words in 10 weeks. It was a stretch; writing a book is different from writing LinkedIn blog posts. During the process, I had to go to the library to do my research, reach out to thought leaders to interview and get feedback along the way. I started by building breadth (divergent) with 34,000 words. After the first round of feedback, I had to expand on one central idea (converge). There was a lot of trimming to do. And I repurposed 50 percent of my content to 18,000 words and built depth on one anchor idea to get the word count back to 34,000 words. Writing this book is an iterative process.

I had to think like an entrepreneur – understanding what problems I am solving (for the readers); validating product market fit; having the speed, cadence and discipline; doing research and feedback; and continuously iterating and improving my writing. These are all parts of being an entrepreneur.

I was totally hands-on, juggling many roles. If you are working in an organisation, you can relate to the various roles listed here:

ROLE	TASKS
Chief Executive Officer (CEO)	Set out the vision for the book (what is it going to do for me and what's in it for the readers), set the tone and build the big idea.
Chief Financial Officer (CFO)	I hold a tight budget. Anything from publishing, marketing and illustration that costs money needs to be reined in.
Chief Product Officer (CPO)	Set the tone, develop the big idea, develop the book structure and start writing. Set the cadence to complete the task and do research to substantiate the writing.
Chief Customer & Marketing Officer (CCMO)	Put the idea to test, get feedback, and adopt an agile and iterative approach to shape the content. I also had to talk to thought leaders; develop a social marketing campaign for pre-launch, launch and post-launch; set up the website; and develop distribution channels and partnerships.
Chief Risk Officer (CRO)	Ensure that everything that is referenced is attributed correctly.

I am sharing this journey with you because in the future of work, agility is important to help us navigate uncertainty ahead. Agility is a hallmark of an entrepreneurial mindset; it helps you become more resourceful, flexible and ready to adapt, regardless of what the current situation is like. Entrepreneurs are nimble; they invest in themselves. They build their professional networks. They take intelligent risks. They make uncertainty and volatility work to their advantage.

Our approach to achieving career success has to change. We will need to navigate our career like an entrepreneur. It is a mindset. Consider the following scenarios:

When you tell others that you want to make what you used to earn by working only 50% of the time,

- **Someone with an employee mindset** will say that's not possible.
- **Someone with an entrepreneurial mindset** will make it happen.

When you are consciously learning new skills from different domains,

- **Someone with an employee mindset** will dismiss this as a waste of time and irrelevant.
- **Others with an entrepreneurial mindset** will create opportunities from this knowledge gained.

When things are going well,

- **Someone with an employee mindset** will say "don't change when things are not broken".
- **Those with an entrepreneurial mindset** will think "let's start looking at new opportunities".

When one door closes,

- **Those with an employee mindset** will wait for another door to open.
- **Those with an entrepreneurial mindset** will create new doors.

If you want to be in the driver seat of your career and life, embrace an entrepreneurial mindset.

These are the very same skills professionals need to get ahead today.

Here are my insights gathered from observing people who have thrived in their careers, from my secondary research and my experience working for a fintech. I also drew on insights from the more than 250 professionals I coached.

Navigate your career like an entrepreneur

One of the best advice I have when it comes to managing your career is to think of it as your own business. By shifting your approach, a new perspective of ownership emerges. What can you do to improve your skill set and develop your professional network? Some of the actions you need to take are:

- Develop learning agility
- Develop strategic side gigs and build range
- Build career lattice
- Invest for your next trajectory when you are still growing

And of course, brand yourself, which I will cover in Chapter 4 Noticeable.

Develop learning agility

Jeff Bezos, founder/executive chairman of Amazon, concludes every annual letter to shareholders by reminding readers as he did in his first annual letter in 1997, that "it's still Day 1" of the organisation: "Though we are optimistic, we must remain vigilant and maintain a sense of urgency". Each day presents an opportunity to learn, do more, be more and grow more in our lives and careers.

In the same way, keeping your career in permanent beta forces you to acknowledge that you have bugs, that there's new development on yourself, that you'll adapt and evolve. This is adopting a growth mindset, as you have the power to improve yourself and improve the world around you.

In a groundbreaking book *Range: Why Generalists Triumph in a Specialized World* by David Epstein, he discovers that in most fields – especially those that are complex and unpredictable – generalists, not specialists are primed to excel. He shows that the way to excel is by sampling widely, gaining a breadth of experiences, taking detours, experimenting relentlessly and juggling many interests – by developing range.

Developing range is about building a set of skills across different disciplines that could augment what you are already doing. It gives you a breadth of perspectives and helps you think outside the box.

When you are developing range, identify what is it that you want to learn. Do a scan in the market to understand what are the rising trends, what kind of skills would be in demand. Seek out skills that are outside of your current professional role. Think long-term.

Based on the World Economic Forum (WEF) Future of Jobs 2020 report, 85% of the jobs that exist in 2030 have not yet been invented. And 50% of employees will need to reskill by 2050. This reinforces the importance for us to continually learn and upskill. Beyond learning, it is also important to find ways to apply your learning.

In my marketing career, I have built a breadth of marketing experiences for example, branding, product marketing, sponsorship and digital marketing. I have also developed depth as each new experience builds on another. Changing industry did give me some range as the operating environment was different and each move stretched my adaptability and developed my learning agility.

Learning agility is a set of complex skills that enable us to learn something new in one place and then apply what we learnt elsewhere, in a wholly different situation. Learning agility is our ability to learn, adapt, unlearn and relearn to keep up with constantly changing conditions.

It's also about being open to new ideas and always keeping up-to-date on the latest trends in the industry. When you're an agile learner, you're comfortable being uncomfortable. Agile learners seek out new challenges, ask for feedback from others to learn and grow, and are reflective. According to the Korn Ferry Institute in the US, learning agility should be considered the single best predictor of an executive leader's success, ranking it above intelligence and education. Companies with the greatest rates of highly agile executives produced 25% higher profit margins compared with peer companies.

I have always been asked whether one should be a specialist or generalist. The notion has become outdated. For us to leapfrog in our career, we need a paradigm shift in our thinking.

In the WEF *Future of Jobs 2020* report, the top three skills of the future are all related to thinking and learning agility. They are:
1. Analytical thinking and innovation.
2. Active learning and learning strategies.
3. Complex problem-solving.

This is why you need to adopt a multi-disciplinary approach in learning to hone your critical thinking and problem-solving skills.

I would also caution here that you must find one skill that you are really good at before you start building range. Having a skill that you are really a genius at and people are willing to pay you for will ensure you have a sustainable career.

I have never really deviated from my core marketing skills; I just build adjacent skills to augment what I do. For example, design thinking is a useful tool as I apply empathy in developing marketing messages and implement a structured approach of test and learn as I build marketing campaigns. I have to develop competency and understanding of technology stacks required to measure campaign performance. I hone my skills as a coach because I believe a good leader needs to be able to coach and build a high-performance team. I keep myself abreast of Web 3.0 because I want to ensure I am always ahead of the curve. These are skills that are outside of marketing but they could one day create new pathways for myself.

Develop strategic side gigs

For most people, side gigs are just side hustles that give them the extra income or an opportunity for them to transit into. But when side gigs are more strategic, it can help you advance your career and ride the waves of change.

I had a client, let's call him David (a pseudonym). He was 39 and a parent to two young children. He got retrenched from his role in mergers and acquisition (M&A) in a consulting firm in 2017 when that sector was experiencing a lull. David was looking to get back to a corporate job. Fortunately while he was in his day job before his retrenchment, he did advisory work on the side for startups – applying his M&A experience to help them in investor pitches and valuation. He was building his network in a different community, expanding his knowledge, experiencing a different culture and building skills in a different area. It was only after he was retrenched that he realised how important his strategic side gig was.

When he was retrenched, the two startups where he provided advisory, offered him a role as a CFO. Although it was at a lower pay than his corporate job, he took up the better offer of the two. The strategic side gig became an interim "lifeline" that gave him the runway to eventually land a better and bigger role in an MNC a year later. During the one year, he learnt a new industry, adapted to a startup culture, built new skills all of which gave him a springboard to a bigger role eventually.

On the other hand, Wendy (a pseudonym), a 42-year-old marketing professional, spent 17 years in the same company she worked at. Although her role had expanded and she was promoted several times in the 17 years, her span of perspectives was limited. Like the fable of the frog in the boiling water, her career was reaching a slow death as she failed to keep up with what's out in the wider market. She was retrenched and prospective employers were concerned about her adaptability. And they were right. She tried a stint in a startup but it didn't work out as she was still very traditional in her thinking. It was an uphill task for two years as she had to unlearn and relearn, shift her mindset and learn to be adaptable. Being an introvert, she didn't build her network and was just contented with her progression in a sunset industry.

These two stories above illustrate the value of developing strategic side gigs. Such opportunities can expand your field of vision and build your knowledge, skills and connections. This goes beyond attending industry conferences and networking events or taking classes at night. I am talking about meaningful engagements that expose you to different people, information and cultures all of which could be synergistic with both your personal interests and your current or future primary work.

In a survey conducted by Ken Banta, founder and principal of The Vanguard Network, he interviewed 122 senior executives from a spectrum of industries. All agreed that outside engagement (as long as there is no conflict of interest) were critical to leadership success today and going forward.

"More than 100 senior executives told us that they considered people's external activities when assessing their fit in succession planning."

Finding the right engagement outside your day job isn't always easy. I am not talking about moonlighting for additional income. The strategic engagements could open the door to many opportunities. And it's those experiences that will become your competitive advantage when you need it.

Build career lattice

Career growth isn't about staying in your lane. The new way of building your career is to build different skill sets along the way – the career lattice. A career lattice is a career progression pathway that could be vertical, horizontal and diagonal in movement. With so many learning options available these days, people are often tempted to simply go to Google, type in some general search terms, and start one of the first courses that pop up. Be intentional about building your career lattice. To ensure relevance, you need to focus on learning the latest emerging skills. You can do this in a couple of ways.

First, track what skills the leaders in your industry are hiring for. Look at recent job postings from the top companies, and see which qualifications keep popping up. Second, reach out to people in your network or on LinkedIn who have the job you want. Talk to people and ask them what they are learning to keep succeeding at their work and what skills they think someone needs to acquire in order to become a viable candidate.

As you get a sense of the most important skills to learn, ask these experts whether they can recommend specific online courses with practical value and not content that is mostly academic insight. For instance, you might seek out instructors who are leading experts in your industry or content created in conjunction with companies that you admire. Look out for the right community to join as well.

Implement learning immediately. So whatever field you're studying, find opportunities to use your new skills. This helps you increase what is called "stickiness".

Learning agility only happens when you are able to apply what you have learnt. For example, I am a certified human-centred design (HCD) practitioner. HCD is a creative approach to problem solving. It is about cultivating deep empathy with people you are designing for, generating ideas, and building prototype, iterating, seeking feedback and improving (FIGURE 2.1). Armed with these tools, I sought out opportunities at work or outside of work to practise.

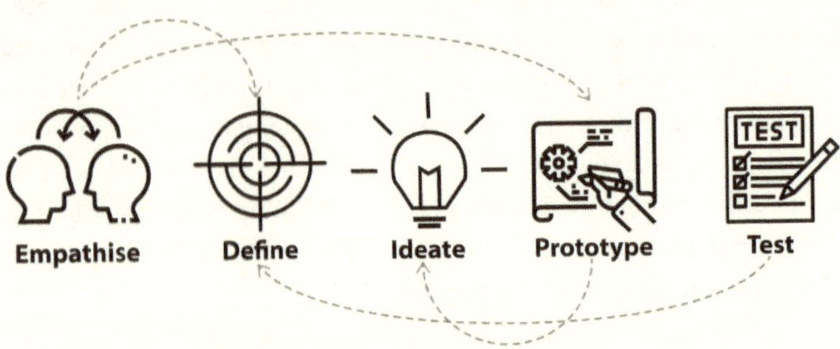

FIGURE 2.1. An illustration of the design thinking process.

I recall in January 2021, a HCD facilitator was down with Covid-19 and could not facilitate an in-person workshop for students at the National University of Singapore. I got to know about it and volunteered to step in. I actually spent the first day of the Lunar New Year, after morning visitations, preparing the slides for the workshop. I had an incredible experience facilitating the workshop of 30 people. Six months later, this led to another opportunity at Ngee Ann Polytechnic, to co-facilitate another workshop of 20 people. That's how I built my experience.

In fact I applied the same design thinking principle when I started writing this book. It is an iterative process in which you seek to understand your users, challenge assumptions, redefine problems and create innovative solutions which you can prototype and test. It is a series of divergent and convergent steps. During divergence, we are creating choices and during convergence, we are making choices.

In design thinking, we have a five-stage process empathising with the problems faced by our target customers, defining the problem statement, and ideating the solutions, prototyping and testing. To illustrate, this is how I wrote my book – after a few chapters, I would test it out with my readers, get feedback and improve on it before I moved on. Sometimes, I worked on a few sections concurrently to shift the sections around to ensure coherency.

Continuous learning is an asset as evident in a 2019 Future of Work Global Survey conducted by GetSmarter. This is a global survey of 8,000 professionals including human resource/learning and development managers, people managers and individual contributors. This research (FIGURE 2.2) shows that individuals who have skills-based certificates on their CVs are also more likely to stand out in the increasingly competitive job market. According to recruiters, they value evidence of continuous learning and learning agility more than anything else when considering candidates.

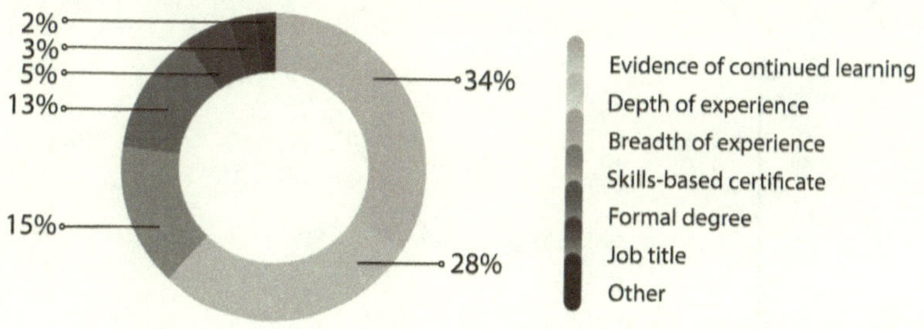

FIGURE 2.2. *Evidence that continued learning is what most employers value.*

The nature of careers is evolving at an increasingly rapid speed as organisations step up on their transformation efforts. As a result, certain roles could look vastly different than they do today in just a few years. This makes the concept of lifelong learning and building adjacent skills an absolute necessity if you want to stay relevant and keep growing in the face of disruption.

Learning new skills can also create different pathways which provide you with multiple streams of income later. And you don't have to trade time and freedom for income. In a very disruptive landscape, no job is secure. I believe it's far riskier not to be diversified; if you are relying on one paycheck from one employer, you may be courting disaster. The old notion of "work hard, get a good job and you'll be rewarded" has changed. Hard work is still important, but today work has shifted towards an ever more independent, work-from-wherever-you-are business economy – accelerated by technology as well as the Covid-19 pandemic. The very idea of what constitutes a career has transformed.

Invest for your next trajectory while you are still growing

The best time to create your new trajectory is when you are still enjoying growth in your current role. We call this the Sigmoid curve (FIGURE 2.3).

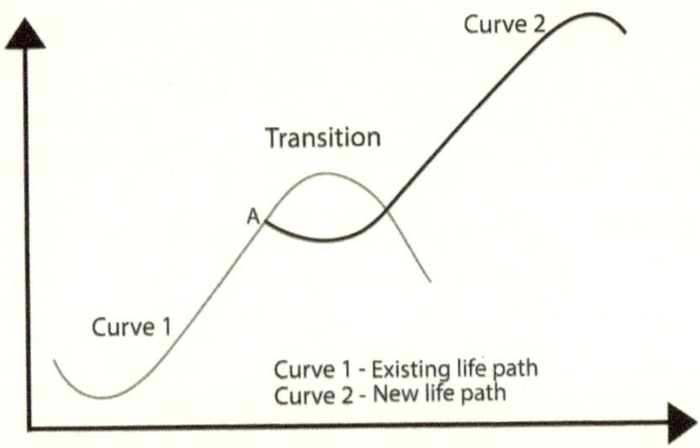

FIGURE 2.3. *The Sigmoid curve.*

It's similar to how CEOs in organisations need to be visionary. The best time to find new growth engines is when your current business matures. History has shown that when organisations are not thinking differently they will become irrelevant. Think how platform players have superseded pipeline business operators. Netflix busted Blockbuster, Apple nuked Nokia, Amazon's Web services upended HP and IBM, and both Google and Facebook (now called Meta) shrank the traditional media industry. It shows that these organisations are too complacent with their own success and failed to disrupt their current business offerings that they vanish into irrelevance.

In the same vein, you are your own CEO. And it is important that you build new pathways as your current role matures. And you want to build skills for the industry of the future. When you have skills for the future, you are in a position of choice. You can choose your work. Don't wait till you are disrupted then you start thinking about what's next. Always stay up-to-date and don't be complacent.

Talent is ageless as long as you continue to demonstrate learning agility and curiosity.

GOING DOWN THE ENTREPRENEURIAL PATH

I first reached out to Elena Chow through a friend. Elena is the founder of a startup. After getting to know her, I was amazed at her entrepreneurial journey. She is an adventure seeker; always taking the path less travelled.

After an illustrious 15-year career in a coveted organisation like Procter & Gamble (P&G), she decided to be a homemaker (after the birth of her fourth child) in 2007. During her career break, a chance encounter gave her the opportunity to mentor startups at the National University of Singapore. This is where she came in contact with the startup ecosystem. During that time, startups were not the most sexiest companies. They were risky and didn't necessarily pay well (it is still so today). People who joined startups are passionate about the cause.

Her career at P&G gave her the opportunity to recruit talents from local universities and build teams. Her passion for developing people was ignited when she mentored the startups. Never one to rest on her laurels, she decided to set up her own talent solutions company in 2013 called ConnectOne, which partnered with early-stage tech startups to build high-performing teams.

For 18 months, the company didn't make money but she felt good about this space. Her entrepreneurial gut convinced her to persevere and work hard on it. Over time, the company won the trust of the community. Today, ConnectOne is the go-to company for recruitment, talent development, leadership and team coaching in the startup community. She was also my "go-to-person" when I needed advice on how to navigate my career in a startup – from building talent to scaling the business.

Elena is constantly evolving. While Web 3.0 is still in its nascent stage, she is accelerating her efforts to build a community of talents to prepare them for the future industry. She invests in the next trajectory while her current business is still growing.

Retirement is not in Elena's vocabulary. To thrive in the future of work, she believes it is important to constantly learn, unlearn and relearn. Her relentless pursuit to excel at what she does and her entrepreneurial mindset contributed to her success today. Life has just gotten richer for her in terms of experience and perspectives.

Asked what her thoughts were on talents that will be sought after in the future of work, she said:

"People need to think beyond a job description or job title. Think like an entrepreneur – what problems can you solve (with the skills you have). You don't need to be an entrepreneur to think like one. Entrepreneurial thinking is a mindset. Taking (calculated) risk, being willing to fail, continuously learning and being highly adaptable to market changes are traits of an entrepreneur.

Entrepreneurs can be highly disruptive (taking risk) as well, thinking outside the box to create innovation. They also have high tenacity and will not let any setback derail their bigger goals. These are the key traits that are important for the future of work."

SUMMARY

In a highly connected world, many jobs are hidden. In fact, hiring managers would trust referrals more than just a fresh resume submission where you are competing in a sea of applicants. So you need to navigate your career like an entrepreneur; build your own network and suss out where upcoming trends are and be able to capitalise on that.

As I write, we are now at the intersection of Web 2.0 and Web 3.0. And I am seeing many new content creators sprouting out content on blockchain, Non-Fungible Tokens (NFTs) and cryptocurrencies on social platforms to establish themselves as thought leaders in Web 3.0. These content creators are being entrepreneurial here in establishing themselves as thought leaders in Web 3.0 and potentially paving new career paths to attract recruiters.

With changes that's happening exponentially and an unpredictable job evolution, being an entrepreneur means you need to adapt fast. Fail fast and learn fast. If Plan A doesn't work, go with Plan B. If all else fails, pivot.

The following are actions you need to take to navigate your career like an entrepreneur:

1. Develop learning agility.
2. Develop strategic side gigs.
3. Build career lattice (instead of focusing on climbing the corporate ladder).
4. Invest for your next trajectory while you are still growing.

Today's long-term career planning is not about knowing exactly where you will be in the future. There is too much uncertainty, unpredictability and change to make specific future plans.

However, just like an entrepreneur, if you build a career that continually expands your experience, skills base, network of connections, mindset and options, then it doesn't matter exactly what changes you will face. You will have the agility, flexibility and adaptability to meet those changes, and build a career and life that makes sense for you.

3 INCLUSIVENESS

"Strength lies in differences, not in similarities."

– Stephen R Covey, author of The 7 Habits of Highly Effective People

A big part of my career is spent building teams and leading them to achieve a collective goal. Over the years, I found myself working with people across different generations – Generation X, Y and Z. At a time when people are living and working longer in a borderless world, a multi-generational and diverse workforce will be a norm. We will experience more diversity in perspectives, conflicts and ambiguities.

Based on US think tank Pew Research Center's article in 2019 on millennials and Generation Z, this decade will see the emergence of a multi-generational workforce (FIGURE 3.1).

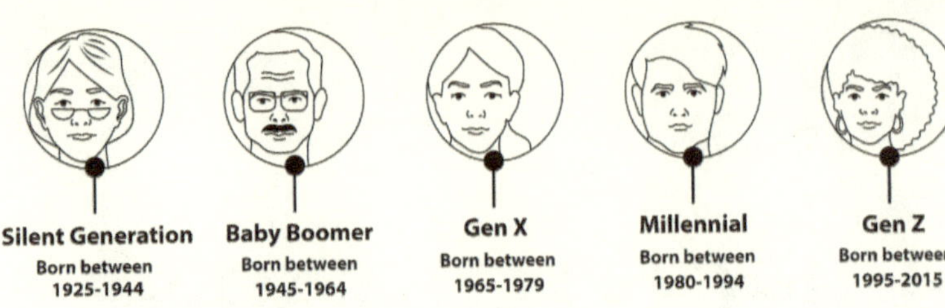

FIGURE 3.1. *Ageing population – the multi-generational workforce in the coming decades.*

There are multi-generations from the silent generation who are born between 1925 to 1944 to Gen Z who are born between 1995 to 2015. This means that we need to equip ourselves with skills to manage diversity, conflict and ambiguity. These arise when we interact with people having different values, communication styles and perspectives.

In late 2020, I wanted to stretch myself. I was looking at how else I could build deeper competency in coaching to help me work better with a diverse group of people. I wanted to find a way to differentiate myself from the sea of coaches out there. I spoke to a fellow coach Suzenne Zheng, an executive life and master neuro-linguistic programming (NLP) coach, one of the best I have known. She's also the founder of First Impression Image International. She specialises in helping people find their differentiation to achieve breakthrough. It was natural that I would consult her.

Me: *Hey Suzenne, there are so many coaches in the market. How do I find a way to differentiate myself?*

Suzenne: *What is unique about you now? (Good coaches always answer you with a question!)*

Me: *I am a marketer, I lead teams and currently, I am also an internal coach for women leaders in the bank.*

Suzenne: *What are you most passionate about?*

Me: *I enjoy building teams and developing people, and I coach them one-on-one.*

Suzenne: *What skills do you think you need?*

Me: *I need the skills to help me manage teams and deal with diversity.*

Suzenne: *Would that be the differentiation you are looking for?*

Me: *Yes, I think that would be a differentiation because I have team and leadership experience that helps me empathise with teams and leaders.*

It was a short but great conversation. That conversation sparked my interest to find out more about team coaching. After some research, I registered for Organization and Relationship Systems Coaching (ORSC) by CRR Global and embarked on a one-year programme of five modules of team coaching workshops. It was timely as my employer at that time, Standard Chartered Bank had just launched a training grant to encourage internal coaches to upskill.

The tools I learned from ORSC give me a head start in leading for the future. There are tools I could use to manage team conflicts more effectively, build a team charter to get better alignment and ask better questions. These tools gave me the dexterity to coach and build a high-performing team.

In the next 10 years, you can expect Generation X, Y, Z and Alpha to co-exist in the workforce. There is also greater expectation on diversity and inclusion. If you are a leader or aspiring to be one, you need to be inclusive and be equipped to embrace – diversity, conflicts and ambiguity. Let's delve into these individually.

Embracing team diversity

Teams are put together to leverage diverse perspectives and expertise. But too often the challenge of integrating diversity in knowledge, skills, perspectives and personality is underestimated and some leaders prefer to take the easy way out.

In a report *Why Diversity Matters* published by McKinsey & Co in May 2020, it finds that companies in the top quartile of gender diversity on executive teams were 25% more likely to experience above-average profitability than peer companies in the fourth quartile.

If you are a corporate executive, you would agree with me that leaders need to embrace diversity and thrive under ambiguity. How many of you would relate to the following scenarios in your workplace when a new or inexperienced manager joins your team?

Scenario	Impact of the team's performance
A new head joins the organisation and tries to manage the existing team out so she can bring her own tribe in	Low morale amongst existing staff and hostile gossip
A manager hires only from the same mould	Lack of diversity, new ideas and all think alike
A leader who sidesteps issues and creates conflict especially those not in his/her good books	Stonewalling by team, apathy and defensiveness
A leader who doesn't communicate and lets the team run their way	Confusion and demotivation

The scenarios can go on. Here's what the outcome looks like in FIGURE 3.2:

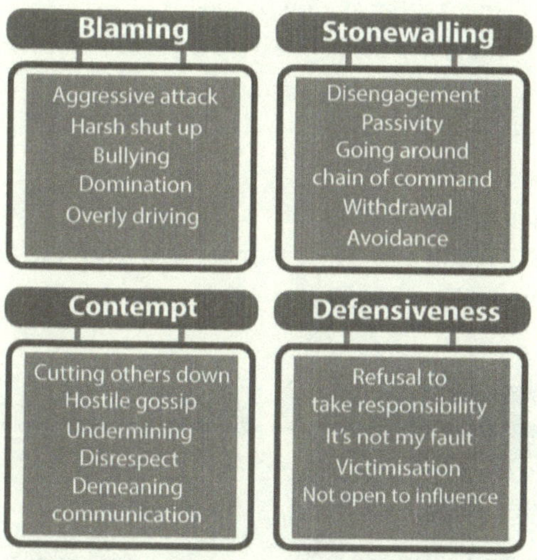

FIGURE 3.2. The toxin grid and behaviours.

These toxin behaviours will lead to low trust and collaboration, a lack of commitment and avoidance of accountability. This will further lead to attrition of the high performers and eventually poor business performance.

One of the tools I use to help bring a diverse team together and build team trust is creating what is called a team alliance. This is when everyone on the team has a say in what kind of culture they want to create and what they are committed to do to create the desired culture and shared success.

There are six questions I would ask and solicit from the team (FIGURE 3.3). In this case the team is considered as a "system" – the collective wisdom of individuals instead of an individual focus.

- This is done with Post-it notes and pens or a mural board (if the work is done virtually).
- We do this one question at a time by first spending 10 minutes to reflect in silence and post it on the board.
- Then everyone takes turns to explain. In this way, everyone on the team has a "voice". It is also useful to understand the rest of the team members and their perspectives on what's good for them.

I had conducted sessions like this and sometimes, it gets emotional when people start sharing their vulnerability and others weigh in to share the support they can give.

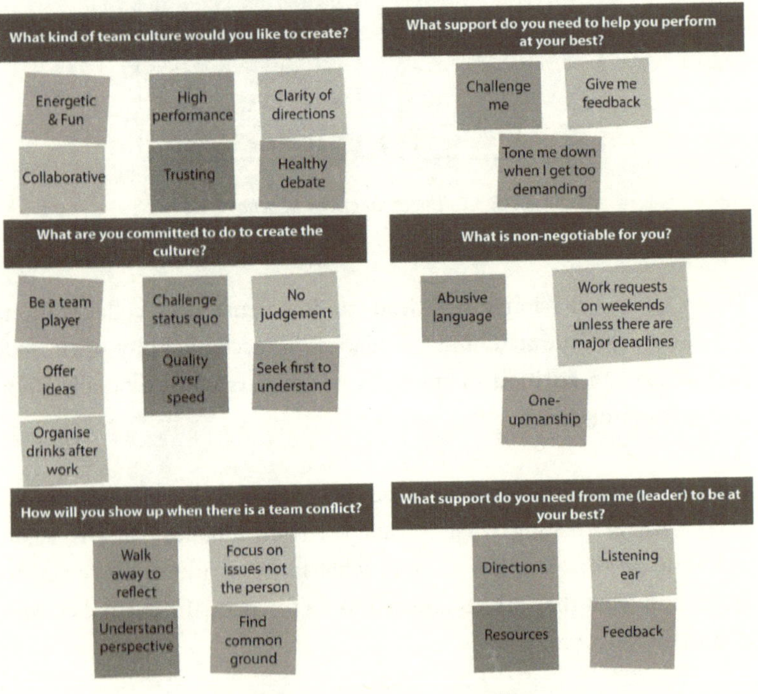

FIGURE 3.3. Building the team alliance.

This is a form of agreement between everyone. It is important to emphasise that it is a safe place to share individual perspectives and call out for support. This charter needs to be revisited regularly if not quarterly, semi-annually as things might have shifted and it is also a good time to calibrate how we show up individually. I find this tool incredibly useful for a start.

There are many forms of a team alliance or charter but these questions provide a good canvas and working agreement.

Embracing conflicts

With a changing and multi-generational workforce, more cross-functional collaborations will lead to conflicts at work as everyone will have their perspectives, and objectives and key results (OKRs) to meet. Being able to manage and embrace conflicts is a skill that is critical for leadership 4.0.

Conflicts could arise due to:

1. **Misalignment of expectations and goals**
   As a leader, you have a huge impact on your teams in terms of expectations – not just on what to achieve but how to achieve it. This can cause tensions within the team as each individual strives to meet the leader's needs.

2. **Disagreements on workflows between the team**
   A difference in opinion on the workflow could slow down progress of projects. This could result in a blame game when timelines are not met.

3. **Differences in work styles and communication**
    When individuals come together into a team, there are inevitably differences in how they work. There are also differences in how they communicate and how they interact.

As a leader, I have had my fair share of dealing with team conflicts. I had once managed the sales, products and marketing teams. There were disagreements on workflows and differences in work styles which resulted in a blame game. For example, the sales team would blame the low sales volume on the slow product delivery. Product team would put the blame on marketing for the lack of creative and impactful marketing, while the marketing team would blame the sales team for not having the competency to close deals.

Each team lead came to me with his/her problems. I had to bring everyone to a common meeting to resolve the conflict. Instead of focusing on each team's problems, I had to re-direct the discussion to focus on:
1. the business targets.
2. the team's commitment to work out the conflicts.

Before I kick-started the meeting, I acknowledged the challenges each team faced. Then I had the team to agree on what they were committed to do to reach a resolution. In managing team conflicts, refocus back on the relationships. I had to wear both a leader and a team coach hat. It's important to set up these premises so they disassociate the conflicts from their own personality. Also, it helps ease the discussion to focus on solutions rather than conflicts.

Each conflict situation as well as team dynamics are different. Many times the conflict arises because we fail to see the other people's perspectives.

When conflicts are managed well, these tensions can serve as a catalyst for creativity, leading to a better employee experience, a higher likelihood of project success, and positive outcomes for the team, corporation and customers.

Embracing ambiguity

Teams today need to be agile, creative and innovative to outperform the competition. Most people experience change as a stressful factor and are challenged by the speed and scope of change. In moments of uncertainty, we tend to operate in a survival mode. The direct consequence of stress in the workplace is that we become less collaborative, less creative and more defensive.

Being able to handle ambiguity is an important competency to lead in 4.0 and key to your career success. The more senior you are, the more likely you are to have to rely on information supplied by others, which may be partial or incomplete. That's when an ability to manage ambiguity becomes a big advantage.

I have encountered many such situations before and over the years as I lead, I have gotten better at it. But with every new organisation I join, there will be new ambiguity and stakeholders to acclimatise to. Here are the time-tested skills I picked up to help me manage ambiguity:

Ask questions

Clarifying questions are the best way to get answers and insights from the unconscious mind. Not everyone is a good communicator and is able to articulate clearly their directions or strategy. Some are simply not sure themselves.

I have resorted to ask (open-ended) questions to help me navigate at work. When I joined a fintech, the solution which was to be launched then was delayed, with no definitive timeline. There were many dependencies.

So I asked my CEO questions at every meet-up:

"What is your priority for the next 90 days?"
"What is required for the solution to be ready? What are the dependencies?
"Where would you like me to focus on in the next 30/60/90 days?
"How can I support your priorities?"

Asking questions helps me eliminate the variables and takes away any ambiguities.

Provide options

To get better clarity, turn those answers into actions. Providing options is a good way to take ambiguity to progress. In many cases, having understood the priorities, there could still be ambiguity and misalignment over what needs to be done.

I have tried to overcome that by offering options. With each option, outline the impact on the business. I use the difficulty and impact matrix to frame my options, steer and influence the decision as illustrated in FIGURE 3.4.

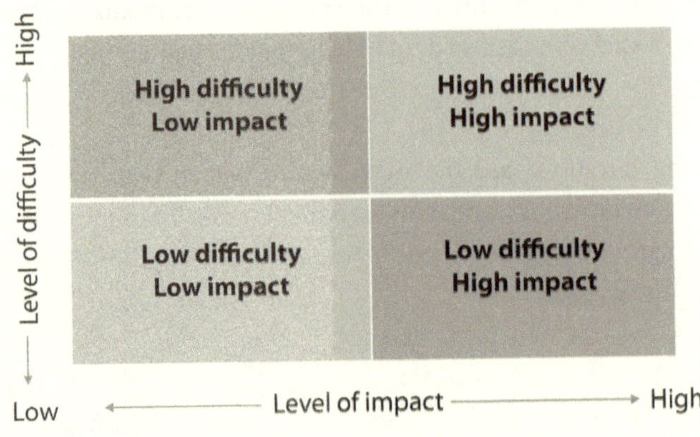

FIGURE 3.4. *The impact and difficulty matrix.*

Small steps

In an environment where there is ambiguity, take small steps so that you will not be stalled. Working in a fintech has immersed me in the agile methodology. When there isn't a full product to be launched, I had to de-risk the business by developing a culture of rapid tests and experimentations.

What this means is ring-fencing your activities, tracking performance (based on the pre-defined metrics) and learning from each small action. In the book, *Atomic Habit: An Easy and Proven Way to Build Good Habits & Break Bad Ones* by James Clear, he shares: "Goals are good for setting a direction, but systems are best to making progress".

Small steps also give you the opportunity to make corrections and pivot; preventing you from big failure later. In this Volatile, Uncertain, Complex and Ambiguous (VUCA) world, progress is more important than perfection. Leaders will need to embrace this and take every opportunity to learn and get better – a practical iterative approach.

Having an inclusive mindset and being equipped with tools to help you embrace diversity, ambiguity and conflicts will give you a competitive advantage in your career.

Here's some practical ways to help you foster a good team culture:

1. **Agree on a set of ground rules or operating principles acceptable to all team members**
   Building the team charter is a tool the team could use to kick-start the discussion. All parties should agree to the charter and take personal accountability. That's how the questions are set up.

2. **Set up regular team huddles for development work**
   This is the time to focus on acknowledging achievements, celebrating small wins and failures, and showing appreciation to individual members.

3. **Put support systems in place to deal, in confidence (if requested), with individuals' troubles or concerns as they arise**

   This way any conflicts that arise can be resolved and not fester into something bigger. Timely feedback is also important so that it is given based on a specific situation and behaviour.

4. **Develop a common interest outside of work**

   Some teams perform better if they strengthen their relationships through shared experience of non-work activities. I have organised bowling sessions and cooking competitions which take the focus away from work and an opportunity to get to know each other. When you build better relationships and find common interests, the teams tend to be more empathetic towards each other.

5. **Learn a new skill together**

   To demonstrate diversity, get each team member to choose a topic they are strong in and would be useful for the team. The team can organise a "lunch and learn" session.

   As an NLP coach, I have run a lunch and learn to get the team to do a preferred learning style test to check if they are visual, kinesthetic, auditory or digital auditory. Then I got everyone to guess each other's learning style through role play.

   I have also gotten team members to share their knowledge on digital marketing, content marketing, etc., to help everyone build their bench strengths.

A TRAILBLAZER WHO ADVOCATES INCLUSIVENESS TO HARNESS VALUE FROM DIVERSITY

I love Ean Yeo's energy. She's an advocate for flexible work arrangements, gerontologist enabler for productive longevity, community builder for women empowerment, trainer and consultant.

She's a mum who keeps reinventing herself and never gives up. With over three decades of corporate experience working with MNCs like Hewlett-Packard (HP) and SME like Xcellink, Ean is now the chief success officer of her own consulting firm.

Her career journey at HP brought her to Hong Kong where she worked in different roles such as sales and marketing, and rose through the ranks. Her exposure in an MNC allowed her to pivot to a SME as a senior leader responsible for employer branding and building good corporate culture. At the SME, she implemented flexible work arrangements to cater to working mothers and those with caregiving responsibilities.

In 2012, she received the Work-Life Harmony Leadership Award by the Singapore government for championing work-life harmony. The pandemic in 2020 further accelerated flexible work arrangements.

Ean's personal mantra is "constantly refresh, redefine and reinvent" to be ready and open to new opportunities. Our lives are no longer linear; priorities and definition of success change at different life stages. A few years back in her late 50s, she decided to pursue a Master's degree in gerontology – the study of the social, cultural, psychological, cognitive and biological aspects of ageing. Her motivation? To prepare herself as she ages and also as a way to contribute back to the society at her life stage.

Having journeyed through various vocations, she has worked with people from different generations. Being part of a multi-generational workforce comes with challenges. Her advice – we need to embrace the new way of working and strive to understand the drivers of work for each generation.

"The Gen Y and Gen Z are likely to be the children of baby boomers and Gen X, respectively. Their expectations of success are different from their parents. Baby boomers or the not-so-savvy Gen Xs must be open to see the value of technology and the new way of working and collaboration. The younger generations need to recognise and have more compassion of the challenges that the earlier generations face especially in the use of technology. It takes both sides to make an effort to change their perspectives so that their synergies can deliver the best results."

Besides a multi-generational workforce, a borderless world also means your colleagues could be from different parts of the world. Ean said: "There is value in this diversity as I have worked across the region and was responsible for building the corporate culture and the employer value proposition in the earlier part of my career. Many organisations are now putting diversity, equity and inclusivity (DEI) as a strategic initiative in the corporate agenda. To thrive, you need to walk the talk and embrace DEI."

SUMMARY

Changing demographics worldwide are creating a labour market in which four generations coexist. For the first time in history, baby boomers, Generation X, millennials (Generation Y), and Generation Z are working side-by-side. With more generations in the workforce than ever before, the workplace values and working styles are changing. Each generation brings with it unique views, experiences, expectations and working styles.

This is one of my favourite quotes – "Strength lies in differences, not in similarities," by Stephen R Covey, author of *The 7 Habits of Highly Effective People*.

To thrive in the future of work, we need to embrace diversity and be able to manage conflicts and ambiguity. Being inclusive and collaborative will increasingly become an important asset for any professional.

4 NOTICEABLE

"Personal branding is about managing your name – even if you don't
own a business – in a world of misinformation, disinformation
and semi-permanent Google records."

– Tim Ferriss, entrepreneur, podcaster and author of
The 4-Hour Workweek

As a professional marketer, I can't complete this book without talking about personal branding and positioning. The skills and experience in building and positioning your company can be equally applied to marketing and branding yourself. As mentioned in Chapter 2 Entrepreneurial thinking, you are the CEO of your personal brand. So it is incredibly important for you to also learn how to brand yourself and be noticed for what you are really good at.

Building a personal branding strategy requires answers to the following questions:

- **Who do you want to serve?** – Your target beneficiaries (this could be organisations) who will benefit from your offerings.
- **What do you want to be known for/what values do you create?** – Your positioning.
- **What is unique about you that differentiates you from others?** – Your unique value proposition.

- **What is your proof point or substantiation for your value proposition?** – Your track record.
- **Why you do what you do?** – Your vision and mission statement.
- **What do you stand for?** – Your value system. This will define your brand personality.
- **How do you show up?** – Your tone of voice and personality that is aligned to your positioning.

The above is a checklist for self-reflection. It's important that you take time to fill in the answers because they will define your communication, partnership and channel strategy. In other words, what you communicate, how you communicate, where you communicate and who you partner to build your brand. Without a clear personal branding strategy, your messaging will be inconsistent or you may even stray off your intent. This will lead to confusion and you will slide into oblivion or worst, add to the noise pollution on social platforms.

So here's five really practical points to take note of.

Build your core competency

Be so good at what you are doing that people cannot ignore you. What if there are many people who are also as good as you are in the same area, how do you become noticeable and stand out from the clutter? There are many ways you can position yourself and find your unique positioning. It doesn't need to be defined by your skills, it can be a specific domain knowledge or a personal trait, or it could be a combination of all.

Let me give you some examples. I once coached a client – a top-notch banker in his 50s who was bankrupt due to his acrimonious divorce. Being a bankrupt meant the end to his banking career in Singapore. But over the years, he built a network of high-net worth (HNW) clients and worked well with clients from a diverse culture.

He had a:

- good understanding of cultural nuances.
- good understanding of the lifestyle preferences for HNW clients.
- won many awards for being the best performer.
- access to HNW clients.

Once he stopped thinking in terms of job functions and focused on capabilities, he had several options. Casinos were happy to meet him because of his access to HNW clients. Concierge companies were keen to hire him to build the businesses to cater to HNW clients. Real-estate companies wanted him on board because they wanted to promote overseas property investments to HNW clients. Even non-profit foundations needed his sales expertise and network to help them raise funds.

In the future of work, we can no longer be defined by job functions. Think in terms of capabilities instead – what value can you bring to the business.

Differentiate and brand yourself

Brand positioning is how you are being perceived in the mind of the prospect. In other words what do you want to be known for? In a sea of competition and information, how can you stand out amongst the other jobseekers who are competing for the same role. You need to position yourself in terms of what value you can bring to the business instead of by your job title. What do you want to be known for and how are you different?

As a consumer you would relate to the following brands and how are they are positioned:

Volvo – Safety

BMW – The Ultimate Driving Experience (focus on how you feel as a driver) for the successful

Mercedes – Success, You have arrived

Starbucks – The Third Place (a place where people gather, outside of home/office)

Cold Storage supermarket – Freshness of Food (they have recently rebranded to CS Fresh to bring the point across strongly)

NTUC FairPrice supermarket – Competitive and good value for daily goods

You can take the same idea to position yourself. For example, you would like to brand yourself as a coach but there are many certified executive coaches in the market. Positioning yourself as an executive coach or even leadership coach is meaningless because your target audience do not know what you can do for them.

Here are some examples of very clear positioning:

From	To
Executive coach/Life coach	Career coach for millennials, Career agility/Clarity coach, Career transition coach
Leadership coach	Leadership agility coach, C-suites leadership coach
Lawyer	Medical lawyer, Intellectual property attorney
Learning & development specialist	Strategic learning and development consultant to SMEs
Chief Marketing Officer	Insights-driven marketer who builds brands and scales businesses

If you can be more specific in your positioning, you are likely to be more focused. Start with a specific detail before you find the right words that best represent your positioning.

It is important to be known for one thing that you are really good at. You want to build your credibility as the go-to-person for a particular value you bring to the business. Conversely as a consumer, would you buy a normal shampoo that cleans your hair or would you buy a shampoo that reduces hair fall, controls dandruff, protects hair colour, etc. Surely, you will buy the shampoo that solves your targetted need.

In FIGURE 4.1, the Tetriminos blocks in Tetris is a good illustration on why it is important to differentiate yourself from the sea of competition. When you are the same as anyone in the crowd, in a competitive job landscape, why would you be shortlisted?

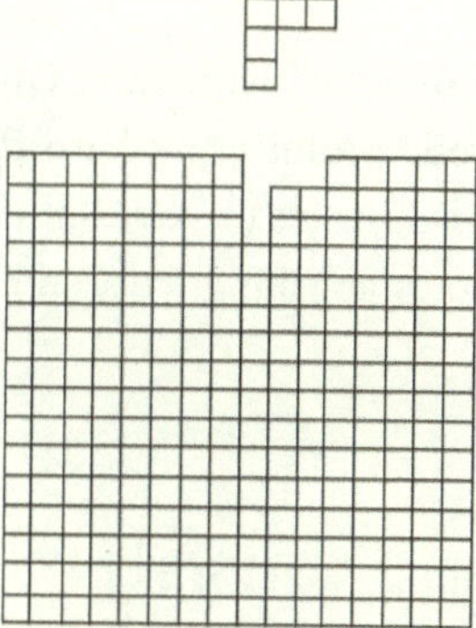

When you try to fit in, you'll disappear.

FIGURE 4.1. The Tetriminos blocks.

Converge perception with reality

As Tesla Motors' CEO Elon Musk once said, brand is just a perception, and perception will match reality over time. It's important that you invest in branding and positioning yourself. But you need to deliver on your promise. Many thought leaders brand themselves on professional network LinkedIn. Keyboard warriors can sometimes get carried away and create a wrong perception of themselves unconsciously without knowing the implication.

At a job interview, I interviewed someone who wrote on his LinkedIn profile "Growth Hacker, Digital Marketer, Data Driven Professional". I then asked him for examples of growth hacking plans and he was not able to even articulate what growth hacking is. He wasn't even familiar with the key metrics for digital marketing. This is a clear example of deception. If the jobseeker is indeed positioning himself as such, he should at least read up to understand what those terms mean. And be able to talk about how brands are leveraging on these techniques to show that he is putting in effort to learn. He could have simply written "Aspiring Growth Hacker". There is nothing wrong with showing humility. Humility is an asset especially when you can demonstrate that you have the right learning attitude.

So use "Fake it till you make it" with care. Once you lose credibility and under-deliver on your promise, it's hard to build back the trust. If people like you, they will listen to you. But if they trust you, they'll do business with you. So establishing trust and keeping to your brand promise is important.

Be authentic and consistent

Technology has blurred the lines between work and personal life. Facebook and Instagram are mainly for non-work related feeds, while LinkedIn is a professional network. However, you are still the same person. Recruiters or prospective business partners can still check you out across the few platforms. The overwhelming majority of employers research potential candidates on social media. More than half of employers have found content on social media that caused them NOT to hire a candidate. Your value system and beliefs should be manifested consistently across your work and non-work social platforms. Also in a highly connected world, people who know you personally can detect your authenticity from what you post online.

Consistency in your branding is important. Which is why the answers to the earlier questions will guide how you execute your brand strategy consistently. For example, I have come across an influencer on LinkedIn marketing herself as a "Personal Branding Coach for C-suites". However she did not demonstrate the credibility in her communication – she would appear on her vblogs, unprofessionally dressed, in dishevelled hair and her blog posts had grammatical errors. Her posturing is not very credible and aligned to her positioning as a coach for C-suites.

So be careful of what content you are putting out on social media.

Establish the right brand partnerships

Brand association is important as "the medium is the message". This is a phrase coined by the Canadian communication theorist Marshall McLuhan to demonstrate that where you place your message is a message of your brand itself. This is probably the most neglected part. Who you associate yourself with says a lot about you. You will need to identify the right "partners" to give you that leverage and work on a win-win. For example, being invited to teach at a university is a validation of your expertise.

In the same way, if you publish a thought leadership article on established platforms, Forbes or Inc, will lend weight to your brand. Find the right platforms that can reinforce your positioning to brand yourself. Or find opportunities to speak alongside industry experts in a subject that is closely related to your positioning.

So it's important to choose the partners that are aligned with your values and positioning or even elevate your positioning if you want to be noticeable.

The same branding and positioning should be extended to be noticeable within the organisation (be consistent both online and offline). Here's a list of what you can do to be more noticeable:

- Build relationships and good rapport with key stakeholders.
- Have a seat at the table – speak up and have a point of view.
- Take on projects that give you opportunities to present to colleagues and management.
- Volunteer or stretch your learning by taking on challenging assignments (when you have fully delivered on what's expected of you).
- Find a sponsor (one with the seniority and authority) within the organisation who can recommend you for opportunities and vouch for you.

SMALL ACTIONS DELIVER BIG RESULTS

I have been following Eric Sim on LinkedIn. He is a banker, lecturer, speaker and author. But I felt that I have known him for a long time. Despite his busy schedule, he has agreed on this interview and for me to share his story here.

He has been very noticeable on LinkedIn, developing and posting content on career success and lifelong learning. What makes him so relatable is his authenticity and good storytelling. As the saying goes "Story sells, data tells". He doesn't brag about his achievements on social media. Instead, he always has a lesson for his followers in every story he tells. I find that requires a deep conviction to create value for his followers. By focusing on what's in it for the audience, he has built a very strong following. In 2020, he was named as a Top Voice on LinkedIn with over two million followers.

Eric, a newly minted author of *Small Actions*, has a very interesting career history and background. A chartered financial analyst, he does not have a "neat" career trajectory. His professional path has had more than its share of bumps, pivots and reset. A Bachelor of Engineering graduate, he has charted his career from corporate sales, and risk management in various banks before becoming a managing director at UBS. Along the way, he created new pathways to teach finance in universities in Hong Kong and Canada. Today, he runs the Institute of Life whose mission is to help professionals achieve success in their careers and life.

In fact, Eric shared in his LinkedIn post how a humble potato actually changed the course of his life. Growing up in a low-income family with near-illiterate parents, he was relatively contented with his small world. "As a kid, my mother would convince me to eat potatoes by telling me kids in other countries were crafting animals and cartoon characters out of them. The next day, I went on the school bus and told the boy next to me – and he not only laughed at me, he stood up and told the whole bus. The other students laughed too."

It then dawned on him that the world he lived in was so tiny. "There was no guarantee that anything I knew was correct." That set him on a quest to verify his knowledge, to keep learning more.

That experience shaped his learning mindset. When he started working, he acquired different knowledge and skills that weren't really relevant to his day job, from art history and graphic design to positive psychology. These "irrelevant" knowledge helped him develop his current career portfolio.

Today, Eric sits at the intersection of several key aspects of the investment world: the C-suite, academia, social media, and networking and mentoring. His career portfolio, which spans five continents, is a diversified one with a host of critical lessons for professionals who aspire to be like him. In navigating his career, he took risks and was entrepreneurial in his thinking – identifying opportunities and the market he could serve. He also developed a system and rigour of self-promotion on LinkedIn to be noticeable so that he could amplify his work and multiply his impact.

His consistency in messaging has also built a strong brand equity. On top of all this, he has developed a strong partnership with LinkedIn which shares similar values for advocating lifelong learning. For his book launch, he partnered with LinkedIn and was able to leverage on the professional network of more than 830 million members in more than 200 countries and territories worldwide to be more noticeable.

His advice – "Start small, start now, stay curious".

SUMMARY

The world is more connected now. Technology has made remote working possible which means talent can be sourced from anywhere in the world. There is more competition for opportunities. In the future of work, it is important that you are able to differentiate and market yourself, and be more noticeable.

Building a personal branding strategy requires very clear answers to the following questions:

- **Who do you want to serve?** – Your target beneficiaries (could be organisations) who will benefit from your offerings.
- **What do you want to be known for/what values do you create?** – Your positioning.
- **What is unique about you that differentiates you from others?** – Your unique value proposition.
- **What is your proof point or substantiation for your value proposition?** – Your track record.
- **Why you do what you do?** – Your vision and mission statement.
- **What do you stand for?** – Your value system. This will define your brand personality.
- **How do you show up?** – Your tone of voice and personality that is aligned to your positioning.

Once you have answered the questions, here are five practical steps for you to be more noticeable:

1. Build your core competency.
2. Differentiate and brand yourself.
3. Converge perception with reality.
4. Be authentic and consistent.
5. Establish the right brand partnerships.

It pays to invest in personal branding to establish your thought leadership in the world of complexity and uncertainty so that you stand out from the crowd. Dare to be different.

5 VULNERABLE

"Courage starts with showing up and letting ourselves be seen."

– Brené Brown, author of Daring Greatly: How the Courage to Be Vulnerable Transforms the Way We Live, Love, Parent, and Lead

What do you think about when you hear the word "vulnerability"? For many of us, the term is linked to negativity, such as weaknesses, personal mistakes or professional danger, or feelings of fear, uncertainty and shame. It's a common misconception. Society has taught us that vulnerability is synonymous with weakness – but author Brené Brown says that it's just the opposite. Vulnerability is the willingness to show up and be seen by others in the face of uncertain outcomes. Vulnerability is about being authentic and being true to yourself.

This new wave of thinking shows that embracing vulnerability is actually crucial to workplace success. While vulnerability comes with the possibility of rejection or failure, which can be scary, there are clear benefits to it such as, it:

- Strengthens relationships.
- Affirms that you are enough.
- Improves self-awareness.

- Fosters learning and growth.
- Gives you courage to speak up or ask for help.

I once coached a client, Kelvin (pseudonym), who was the head of business enterprise at a local SME. He maintained his privacy and only focused on work with minimal social interactions. He viewed his position as not getting too personally involved with employees – he was stoic and poised at work and behaved in a fairly robotic manner. His colleagues ended up trying to read his mind, and making assumptions, which could be totally wrong. After some coaching, Kelvin became more authentic and open to sharing. He started talking more about his family, interests and emotions at work; instead of being a personality-less leader, he added dimensions that allow him to connect with his colleagues. Nearly as soon as Kelvin started to embrace authenticity and show his personal side, he noticed that his colleagues were more engaged and productive around him. Instead of just being the boss, Kelvin could build connections with other colleagues and improve everyone's work experience and the overall team culture.

Keep it real

Everyone has vulnerabilities, emotions and personality components that are either good or bad. By hiding those vulnerabilities, you are essentially denying a major part of your personality. Vulnerability allows you to connect on a different level, which can lead to increased collaboration, productivity and cohesiveness. Being vulnerable means taking a risk, which can be daunting for you to do, but when everyone at work feels comfortable taking the vulnerability plunge, everyone can benefit. This can only happen when there is psychological safety at the workplace.

Embracing vulnerability can look different for each of us. Start by thinking about who you are at work and who you are at home – are they the same person? Most people let themselves relax and be comfortable at home, so try to embrace those same principles at work to be authentic to your true self. Being vulnerable doesn't mean you have to "tell it all". You will need to preserve and respect your level of privacy.

Next, use that personality for real conversations. People want to work with a human, not a robot, and most people are excited to talk about their personal lives and emotions, either good or bad. Build connections with co-workers through real, honest conversations. It could be a travel experience, a mishap, an adventure or a learning experience. Stories connect and make you relatable. Having open, non-judgemental conversations fosters an environment of cohesiveness and teamwork.

This may sound counterintuitive.

When I have conversations with my team, I often ask them to think two steps ahead and plan where they want to be beyond their current role. Even if I don't initiate such conversations, they would look out on their own anyway. Then I would ask them to reflect and review if their timeline to achieving their career aspirations is aligned with their progress in their current role. Of course, whenever possible, I would create the opportunities and career pathway to help them grow within the organisation.

But more importantly, I would remind them that they are their own CEO and to adopt entrepreneurial thinking in managing their career. That shift usually gives a lift in their intrinsic motivation at work. If they continue to stay on my team, I get a more motivated and high-performing individual. If they leave the organisation, I make a good friend.

Authenticity and openness help conversations thrive.

Having said that, recently there was a case of a CEO who captured a selfie of himself in tears after he just retrenched his company's staff. He expressed his vulnerability and that he felt bad about the exercise.

His post on LinkedIn received many backlashes as it seemed the vulnerability was being carried overboard or fake. They felt that if he was truly sad and compassionate, he could have reached out on social media to ask for job opportunities for his retrenched staff.

People can detect authenticity intuitively. So be authentically human.

Know when not to overshare

While being vulnerable and authentic builds better connections, you need to find the right balance between sharing and oversharing. This is not easy. A good rule of thumb for figuring out if you are sharing too much is to ask yourself – "How would I feel if my manager said this to me?" If it's something that you'd be thankful to hear, chances are your team would feel the same. Be aware of your intentions. Are you sharing from a place of authenticity, or just trying to fabricate a connection with others? Sometimes, we overshare our personal experience just to feel close with someone else, which may not be useful. Be selectively vulnerable.

For example, if you are a leader saying – "I'm scared, and I have no idea what to do right now" – there is a good chance your colleagues will take on that same emotion, or worse, lose faith in your ability to lead. People in charge have to think long and hard than the rest of us about when to be transparent because they have more eyes on them.

Another way to balance your sharing and setting the boundaries is to acknowledge your feelings without being too emotional. "The idea that you're never going to have a bad day as a boss is bullshit," mentions Kim Scott, author of *Radical Candor: Be a Kick-Ass Boss Without Losing Your Humanity*. "The best thing to do is to cop to it. Say to your team, 'I'm having a bad day, and I'm trying my best not to take it out on you. But if it seems like I'm having a bad day, I am. But it's not because of you that I'm having a bad day. The last thing I want is for my bad day make your day worse." In this case acknowledging your feelings helps you avoid creating unnecessary anxiety among your colleagues.

Striking the balance is not easy. But with practice, it can be done.

Embrace imperfections

Life is filled with comparisons. We see celebrities who seem to have everything we could ever want. Our friends on social media always look like they are so much more successful, attractive or interesting than we are. We hear about people finishing school early, working at an esteemed company, or starting their own impressive business. In comparing ourselves to others, we often fall short. We aim for perfection for everything – the perfect job, family, body and house, you name it.

Embracing imperfection is easier said than done. The first step to do is to recognise where perfectionism exists in your life. From there, reflect on those areas, and ask why the pressure exists. Do you feel pressure from society? Do you fear failure if you do not achieve certain goals? Is your feeling of worth tied to this?

Here are three things you can do to overcome your urge to be perfect:

- **Letting go** – perfectionism has to do with how you want to be seen i.e. perfect. But that is an unattainable goal because you have absolutely no influence on how you are seen by others. So let go and be yourself.
- **Good is good enough** – focus on efforts rather than results. Sometimes when we focus on the outcome, we fail to recognise what went wrong in the process to help us improve. Embracing imperfections also demonstrates humility.
- **Taking (calibrated) risks every now and then** – when you let go of the need to be perfect, you are more willing to take risks and are

prepared to fail. When you experiment and take some risks, you may also arrive at new ideas and creative insights.

When you embrace imperfections, you will feel like:

- Having the freedom to pursue the goals that you truly want to achieve.
- You are always learning through your mistakes as you reflect on them.
- Being able to recognise and celebrate your strengths and accomplishments.
- Being more compassionate and kind to the imperfections of others.

Letting go of the pressure to be perfect can be freeing. In learning to accept ourselves as imperfect, we can take some pressure off ourselves and enjoy more of our present. These are good feelings that will make you antifragile as you go through many inflection points in your lifetime.

Bounce back from setback

In the real world (not metaverse world), whether you like it or not, you're bound to run into setbacks and stumbles throughout your career. Whether you are passed over for a promotion (despite your hard work and stellar performance), retrenched or failed in a business venture, every setback is a learning opportunity and a psychological strengthening exercise. Someone who has a too sheltered career may have a very unrealistic lens to the future of work and lack perspective. When I reflected on my past failures, I realised something: they didn't destroy me. In fact, they were like primers preparing me for something bigger.

In fact, every setback could be a turning point in your life, depending on how you choose to respond to it. Acknowledge the situation and reframe "failure". Somewhere along in my career, I had a new boss who parachuted in from an advertising agency. She had never managed a team before and suddenly in the new role she had to helm a department of 30 people. And I was one of the direct reports. Lacking the experience and feeling insecure, she wanted to bring in staff from an advertising agency (same mould as her). She started putting most of her direct reports on a performance improvement plan, including myself. Most of the other people left but I prevailed. I delivered on all the targets she set as part of the plan. Six months later, I was offered a bigger role within the organisation by another business head who recognised my value. That subsequent role paved the way for my next career trajectory. I am glad I persevered as I would not have a story to tell.

Failure is an event, not a person. Every inflection can create the momentum for greater success. It's ok to be less than perfect. Being vulnerable makes you human.

WHEN LIFE GIVES YOU LEMONS, MAKE LEMONADE

When it comes to the trait vulnerability, one name keeps popping up in my mind. I met Eugene Seah, a mindset speaker and abundance life coach, and TEDx speaker in 2017 when I was on a career break and attended his personal branding workshop. Although I am a corporate branding specialist, I felt what he taught in class was refreshing – using a personal story to connect.

His story:

He was retrenched from his high-flying job in 2014, a setback that forced him to reflect, recalibrate and reset. As the sole breadwinner to a family of five, the loss of income was hard on him that he had to go on social service support and resorted to borrowing money from his brother residing in the US.

He was working in Hong Kong then and his family was getting used to the expat lifestyle. But that disruption changed everything.

His family had to relocate back to Singapore not too long after. Suddenly pride turned into shame.

"I felt shameful and lied to my friends that I didn't like the life in Hong Kong. I lied for one year and that burden got heavier on my shoulders. I was also getting confused as some close friends knew the truth and some didn't. The guilt and confusion affected my mental well-being."

One day, Eugene decided to write a long post on Facebook to reveal the truth. That confession immediately liberated him. To his surprise, many reached out to him to offer emotional support and some even offered ideas to bounce back.

That freedom gave him the drive and momentum to start from a clean slate. He took the opportunity to reinvent himself and started his training, coaching practice and also became a certified financial advisor. In 2020, he was named one of the Top 5 life coaches in Singapore. He also achieved the Million Dollar Round Table award every year from 2018 to 2022. This is a prestigious award given to the top 5% of financial advisors in the world.

Success didn't come easy. In the initial years, he started his training business focusing on schoolkids. The business was seasonal and he had to put food on the table. He did a lot of hustles – offered free coaching, ran training workshops at special discounts and spoke at events for free.

His authenticity and generosity to keep giving pays back manifold. Today, he is a highly sought after motivational speaker internationally.

Vulnerability is a measure of authenticity and courage. Conventionally vulnerability is a sign of weakness. Eugene has shown that vulnerability strengthens relationships (he is real!). It has also helped him reconnect with himself, and given him the courage to speak up and the momentum to achieve his bigger calling. Because of his willingness to share his setback, he has normalised conversations on retrenchment, which has attracted many media interviews and coverage. In fact in the larger scheme of things, a retrenchment is just a bump in a lifelong adventure and is an opportunity to reset.

Today, he champions the "abundance" movement. He has a deep conviction that we have more than enough in life to live a purposeful and fulfilling life. By embracing an abundance mindset, we become more generous and charitable. By focusing on giving, we get more in return in terms of goodwill, happiness and prosperity.

By embracing vulnerability and imperfection, he is also more understanding of others. But Eugene continues to set a high bar for himself and those around him. As he shared, "Life is a self-fulfilling prophecy. You achieve what you believe."

Despite his busy schedule, he readily agreed to support me for this interview. I took the opportunity to ask him – what is the most important trait to be successful in the future of work?

"The antifragile mindset. This is a concept populated by essayist Nassim Nicholas Taleb. Antifragile is about the ability to bounce back stronger from each crisis. It's just like muscles. They grow stronger after going through stress. In the future of work, you need to be open to fail and learn from it."

SUMMARY

Being vulnerable makes you more relatable to others and compassionate towards yourself and others. These strengths will keep you anchored through the waves of transformation and protect your mental well-being.

To sum up, these are the benefits of being vulnerable:

- Strengthens relationships.
- Affirms that you are enough.
- Improves self-awareness.
- Fosters learning and growth.
- Gives you courage to speak up/ask for help.

Vulnerability is still somewhat of a taboo term in many workplaces. However, when you know how to capitalise on your vulnerabilities and bring your real-self to work, you create an environment of trust, growth, respect and opportunities for better connections. These are all important factors for success in the future of work.

6 EMPATHY

"Empathy represents the foundation skill for all the social
competencies important for work."

– Daniel Goleman, author of Emotional Intelligence:
Why It Can Matter More Than IQ

The Covid-19 pandemic has exacerbated issues of work-life balance, financial pressures and fears about job security. On top of that, the Ukraine war in 2022 and geopolitical tension between US and China are also having further ramifications on the world economy and fuelling people's fears about their future. In a global employee experience study by Qualtrics in early April 2020 (of more than 2,000 employees from Australia, France, Germany, New Zealand, Singapore, UK and US), two in five (41.6%) respondents said their mental health had declined since the outbreak of Covid-19, while 57.2% reported higher levels of anxiety.

Organisations are now prioritising mental well-being in their corporate culture to address these problems to prevent talent leakage. And if you are leading teams, empathy can increase your team engagement, deepen trust while driving greater innovation and growth for the organisation.

I have been leading teams for more than 15 years. No amount of reading or training will prepare you to lead. I get my best leadership lessons from my own failures as well as working for terrible bosses. As the saying goes, "You learn more from failure than from success". Failure builds character. Collectively, the lessons shaped how I lead.

Getting myself certified as a coach was pivotal in my development. As a task-oriented person, coaching has provided me the balance and developed the empathy in me. Empathy can create better psychological safety, and drive innovation and engagement. Leaders who are more empathetic can have great impact on businesses.

In a US research by Catalyst called *Leveraging Disruption for Equity*, it highlights the negative impact unempathetic leadership can have on a company's performance:

- 61% of people surveyed with highly empathic senior leaders report often or always being **innovative at work** compared to only 13% of those with less empathic senior leaders.
- 76% of people surveyed with highly empathic senior leaders report often or always **feeling engaged**, compared to only 32% of those with less empathic senior leaders.

Empathy is not a "nice to have" or something that is warm and fuzzy that makes you feel good as a leader. Empathy is a valuable attribute that enhances overall cooperation, respect and understanding. By cultivating empathy, we are better equipped to make connections across cultures.

How do you develop empathy? Here's four actions you can consciously take to build your empathy muscles:

Watch out for unconscious bias

Like it or not, bias remains a big issue in the world of work. Some biases are conscious – meaning we are aware of our own feelings towards a certain person. These biases can be called prejudices which you can change.

Unconscious biases are biases that are ingrained in our psyches and influence our decision-making and how we treat others. At the workplace, it influences our decisions around recruitment, recognition and career progression. The result is situations where certain people are favoured over others. How often have you experienced extroverts being perceived as higher achievers compared to the quiet introverts?

Here are some examples of unconscious biases:

- **Affinity bias** – feeling a connection to those similar to us. For example: believing that someone is a 'good fit' for your team because you are of a similar age or socioeconomic background, or viewing someone as particularly intelligent because you attended the same university.
- **Perception bias** – stereotypes and assumptions about different groups. For example: a team member doesn't invite another teammate to an after-work social event because he/she assumed that the teammate wouldn't share similar interests with the overall group.
- **Halo effect** – projecting positive qualities onto people without actually knowing them. For example: when one assumes that a good-looking person in a photograph is also an overall good person.
- **Confirmation bias** – looking to confirm our own opinions and pre-existing ideas. For example: believing that left-handed people are more creative than right-handed people.

These biases undermine trust and erode empathy. To be empathetic, we need to understand other's perspectives and put ourselves in their shoes. If we already have assumptions or pre-conceived ideas about the person, it would cloud our decision-making.

Ageism is real. But one of the clients I had coached showed that talent is ageless.

I once coached two clients of similar career profile and age. They were both experienced communication specialists. Let's call them Jane and Angela, pseudonyms.

Jane came to see me feeling dejected and resigned to the fact that at 52 years old, she faced perception bias from hiring managers. Angela, however invested in upskilling herself, and learned coding and digital marketing. She was also actively building her network and doing pro-bono work such as writing media releases for her church. By staying active and current, she was able to demonstrate her value to the organisation. At 53 years old, she was eventually hired and offered a similar role with a pay increment. This was despite a career break of four years to look after her ageing mother. She worked hard to overcome the perception bias. Hiring managers looked beyond her age and appreciated the value she brought to the role.

This is unlike Jane, who just accepted the bias and never got back to a job at her level.

Letting go of the need to win

Humility is a leadership superpower. It is about knowing what you don't know and having the curiosity, authenticity and confidence to put that out there so that you and your team can find the answers.

When I first became a line manager at 26 years old, humility was not one of my traits. Highly ambitious and a go-getter, my focus was always to stay ahead of my peers. It gave me tremendous satisfaction to "win".

And at that time, to win, I made sure I recruited team members who were good or even better than me. The motivation was to show that I had a high-calibre team and push myself to grow in my leadership. That streak of competitiveness created the perception that I was arrogant and not a collaborator.

As a result, I was passed over for promotion. A lesson that was humbling. In the future of work, organisations are advocating more cross-functional collaboration, which means team leadership is not just limited to vertical teams. You will need to have constructive conversations with your peers, break down walls and work collaboratively.

Let go of the need to win and learn to ditch the "know it all" mindset. When you focus less on winning and be open-minded, you will listen and be more empathetic.

Ditch the task and be present

Today's professionals feel rushed and overwhelmed. We are time-starved. We keep our heads down, focused on achieving the next thing, and the next without a moment to breathe or even spare a thought for others.

You need to remind yourself to slow down. Make an effort to see things from others' perspectives. Avoid multi-tasking especially when it comes to writing emails. You may unconsciously set an unreasonable timeline or make an unrealistic request. These may come across as over-imposing, despite your best intentions.

In the same way, when you meet someone new, ask how they are doing and what their life is like. People like to talk about themselves. Recognise what makes them passionate, happy and sad. Meaningful conversations will lead to a long-term relationship. Be fully present and resist the temptation to check your phone. It takes a very conscious effort but over time, you are wired to be more empathetic.

And when interacting with someone, consider what is called "empathic listening". It is basically being present in the moment and hearing someone else's story without the need to judge or react. It requires compassion, curiosity and a willingness to be open to what the person is saying. It is worth it. Practising empathic listening regularly can lead to meaningful connections with others and improved emotional well-being.

Lead with your heart

The first value in the agile manifesto is "people and interactions over processes and tools". In this digital age, work relationships are ever more important. Authentic, trust-based relationships will increase job satisfaction, leading to greater engagement, higher productivity, longer employee retention, and even decreased healthcare costs.

Here's six reasons why empathy is important for your future success:

1. **You will be able to work more effectively with others**
   a. Empathy helps us develop a deep level of rapport and trust at work and in our personal lives.
   b. You will understand how you affect others. By understanding another person's viewpoint, you can evaluate more clearly how your words and actions will affect and influence them.
2. **You will be better equipped to deal with interpersonal conflict**
   Understanding another person's perspective will help you in both professional and personal relationships. It would be easier for you to resolve any potential conflicts.
3. **You will more accurately predict people's behaviour**
   Because you focus on what motivates people's behaviour, you'll

be better able to understand how to interact with the people you work with.

4. **You will be better at understanding non-verbal cues**

   Your sensory acuity will be sharp and you will be better equipped to understand unspoken communications with others. Hence, you will improve your interactions with people in the workplace or in social spaces.

5. **You will be better at motivating others**

   By understanding what drives others and what they want to achieve, you can inspire and motivate them better.

6. **You will be able to look at the bigger picture**

   When you incorporate different perspectives or worldviews, you'll be able to see the bigger picture of an issue or concept.

Covid-19 has disrupted our work and life, affecting our well-being as we try to cope. It has caused many to reflect on their priorities and purpose. In the face of these disruptions, being empathetic towards yourself and those around you will ease any anxiety caused by the disruptions. We all need a strong mental and emotional resilience to ride the waves of changes ahead of us.

A THRIVING HORIZON CHASER, TRANSFORMING PEOPLE'S LIVES

I first came across Chin Sau Yong's profile on LinkedIn in 2020 and was very intrigued with the diversity of his experience and skills. He calls himself a "horizon chaser, people developer and T.H.R.I.V.E advocate". A commercial pilot since 2007, he is also an active coach. In fact, he got himself certified as a Gallup CliftonStrengths coach, co-founded and launched the T.H.R.I.V.E (acronym for Thoughts, Health, Relationships, Income, Vocation and Enlighted self-awareness) initiative. This is a movement to build and enhance holistic resilience. He also co-wrote a book of short stories and poems to raise money for charity, and hosts an on-going LinkedIn

Live series called "Chasing Horizons" to inspire people to achieve their dreams. He does all these when he is not flying.

He exemplifies someone who is agile and entrepreneurial – the key traits that are important for the future of work. When the pandemic reduced his flying time during the two years, he took the opportunity to build new skills such as coaching. In fact, these skills augment what he does professionally. Within the airline, he is also actively involved in the development of human-centric skills of pilots – the non-technical competencies required for aviation such as leadership, decision-making, communication, teamwork and situational awareness. You would want to fly with a pilot who demonstrates a strong ability to lead and make decisions in times of crisis. Coaching has also empowered him to create better psychological safety in his workplace.

I had a chat with him about how coaching has helped him in his relationships.

"Coaching has been a transformative skill when it comes to relationships as it has allowed me to engage and connect more deeply with the people around me. Whether it's a personal or professional context, the ability to listen effectively, pick up non-verbal cues and ask meaningful questions allows me to uncover the heart of the matter. I am more empathetic with people around me. This has brought me closer to my loved ones. It has also helped me become a better leader at work, helping to iron out any conflicts or issues."

By expanding his skill sets, he has also expanded his network to a larger community beyond pilots. The larger network gave him different perspectives and experiences, all of which help him improve his coaching. He is also an astute marketer and influencer on LinkedIn, which further expands his network as he is more noticeable.

Sau Yong has just reinvented himself by building new capability that meets a market demand. Flying the plane and coaching may sound totally unrelated, but this is an adjacent skill that enhances what he does professionally. As the captain of a commercial flight, he needs to be empathetic towards the passengers and cabin crew to ensure a positive experience on a flight.

SUMMARY

Empathy is an important ability for everyone. It helps us understand and relate to people from all walks of life or from different generations. It improves your capacity to communicate with others, to be part of a team and to better your leadership skills. This is becoming one of the most important traits for the 21st century.

Here's what you can do to build your ability to empathise:

1. Watch out for unconscious bias.
2. Let go of the need to win.
3. Ditch the task and be present.
4. Lead from your heart.

In the future of work where we have multi-generations in a team, empathy is important for your future success. And this is a skill that will never be replaced by robots.

7 NETWORKING SKILLS

"Networking that matters is helping people achieve their goals."

– *Seth Godin, author of* Purple Cow: Transform Your Business
by Being Remarkable

Like many of us, I used to be turned off by the topic – networking. I used to think it felt sleazy and inauthentic. Imagine the consummate networker – the high-energy fast-talker who collects as many name cards as he can, and attends networking mixers in the evenings. These old-school "networkers" are transactional. They pursue relationships thinking only about what other people can do for them. And they will only network with people when they need something, like a job or new clients.

Because of my job as a marketer, I have learnt to network. As an introvert, I don't like small talk. So I changed my paradigm of networking. I focus on building relationships, intentionally. I try to help other people achieve their goals. I don't keep score. But I know that many good deeds will be reciprocated in the future in the most unexpected ways. I prioritise high-quality relationships over a large number of connections. Strangers who reach out to me especially via LinkedIn and request a meet-up without a specific ask, won't get a response from me. I don't pretend to be the consummate networker.

To build meaningful networks and genuine relationships, you need at least these two things. The first is seeing things from the other person's perspective. When you truly put yourself in the other person's shoes, you begin to develop an honest connection. The second requirement is thinking about how you can help and collaborate with the other person rather than what you can get from him/her.

Build a strategic network

I wrote about building a range of skills and knowledge in the earlier part of the book. That is building your intellectual capital. But investing in social capital – your network is equally important in the future of work. With LinkedIn, Facebook, Telegram and others, most people are easily connected and good careers are mainly found through these networks.

Investing in social capital is not about increasing your network, but spending time to nurture meaningful relationships. Just think of it as the emergency funds in the bank account. If you start depositing in the emotional bank account, you can draw on them when you need them the most.

Here are two different situations of clients whom I have coached and how a network made a difference:

John Ng (pseudonym), 54 years old, had just returned from a nine-year stint in China. The business in China didn't work out and he decided to return to Singapore to find a job. He used to work at Government Linked Companies (GLCs) in very senior roles like senior vice-president. He had a very illustrious career in the GLCs and an impressive resume. During our coaching conversations, he went through his list of contacts whom he could reach out to explore opportunities. There were 10 on his list. He came back after a few weeks and shared that none of the meetings turned into a job opportunity because they found him too senior and there were no roles available at the moment. We tried exploring other options like attending networking events and developing his elevator pitch. At the end, he decided to resort to driving Grab to occupy his time. Driving Grab did not help him build new skills. But perhaps, his strategy was to hopefully pick up a CEO who was hiring. What are the odds in that happening?

Then there is Kenneth Long (pseudonym), also 54 years old, who had come back from a long employment in China. He had worked with several SME and MNCs in Singapore before a 10-year stint in China. When he first met me, he shared that he had to rebuild his network in Singapore from scratch. He was actively reaching out to his network for coffee. His intention was not to look for a job as he knew that a rekindled relationship needs to be nurtured. Sometimes a network could give him new insights and referrals to help in his search. He was strategic in his job search and thinking long-term. After six months, he landed a new role, which was a stepping stone to his dream job.

The two scenarios illustrate that we need to continually invest in building our social capital. As the saying goes – your network is your networth.

Dorie Clark, author of *The Long Game: How to Be a Long-Term Thinker in a Short-Term World*, advocates the best form of networking is to adopt an infinite horizon. It's pure, no-agenda relationship-building. Because you have zero goals or expectations – only a fundamental interest in who the person is – you can enjoy the experience and let it unfold naturally. In building your network, the person you first meet may have no professional relevance to you such as you're a marketer and they're accountants, or you're a journalist and they're business owners. But given enough time, career and life trajectories may change, and your path could surprisingly converge. So start investing for the long-term.

Tap on your professional allies

Jane Ho (pseudonym), a human resource practitioner, took some time off work to look after her elderly parents until their passing. By then she was six years out of work. But fortunately, during that time, she kept in touch with fellow practitioners in the community. Some of them had also left the workforce and came back again so they could empathise with Jane. When she was ready to get back to work, she tapped on her professional allies to understand where the opportunities were.

By doing so, she also understood how the role of human resource had evolved and was aware of her skill gaps. So she took the next six months preparing to get back to the workforce by attending the appropriate classes to bridge the skill gaps. So when an opportunity came, she was ready to take on the role with a pay increment.

Expand the breadth of your network

Relationships are living, breathing things. Feed, nurture and care about them, and they will grow. Neglect them, they die. This is like growing the "starters" for your sourdough bread. Weak ties in a career context were formally researched in 1973, when American sociologist Mark Granovetter asked a random sample of Boston professionals who had just switched jobs, how they found their new jobs. Of those who said they found jobs through a contact, Granovetter then asked how frequently they saw the contact.

About 16% of the recipients said they found their job through a contact they saw often. The rest found their job through a contact they saw occasionally (55%) or rarely (27%). In other words, the contacts who referred jobs were "weak ties". He summed up his conclusion in a paper appropriately called "The Strength of Weak Ties": the friends you don't know very well are the ones who refer winning jobs. So it is good to expand the breadth of your network because any contacts whether weak or not may end up providing good leads.

For example, I met Kenny, a fellow mentor at a mentoring social enterprise. We came from diverse backgrounds. Later when he knew that I was on a career break and getting my coaching certification, he recommended me a role at a career-matching provider. That's where I got to coach more than 250 clients over 15 months. Another person, I got to meet was Cindi from a women's network. When I found out that she was facilitating a team building workshop, I provided her with the tools that I learnt from my team coaching certification. Sometime later, she referred me to a speaking engagement at a public event. I have also advanced my career in the last two decades all thanks to many others in my network.

Set up a "networking" fund

I am sure you would agree on the power of a network. But will you actually follow through? Just like you set aside budget for your family vacation, you can set aside a fund for networking or "interesting people" fund. Enacting behavioural change isn't easy. Start with taking small steps. Use the fund to pay for coffee, lunches or even the occasional plane ticket to meet new people and shore up existing relationships. By doing so, you are indirectly investing in yourself. It's not just the people you know. It's the people they know – your second- and third-degree connections. You can even plan an event where your friends bring a few of their friends and invite your extended network. And when you meet someone new at an event, don't forget to follow-up after. Simple gestures like a thank-you note or following up on something you had talked about.

Technology has democratised professional connections. Look through your online professional network, LinkedIn. Identify some interesting people to meet up. Find common ground or interest to nurture the relationship. Show a genuine interest in getting to know the person. Commit to trying to help him/her proactively by giving small gifts – it can be an interesting article, or forwarding a job posting. Invest serious time and energy in the relationship over several months. It is like making a deposit. Imagine you got laid off from your job today, who are the people you'd email to solicit their advice on what to do next?

Networking as an introvert

Extroverts are natural social butterflies and they can move from one conversation to another seamlessly. What happens if you are an introvert? How do you work the room? Introverts and extroverts are wired to recharge and relax differently. Introverts can be effective networkers too. They do better on a one-to-one setting. If you are an introvert, leverage on this strength to build meaningful conversations. Do your prep work before these events and identify who you want to connect with, prepare a list of ice-breaker questions and your elevator pitch. This preparatory work will take away the anxiety and social awkwardness. I am an introvert so these tips give me more confidence to engage. In addition, being a marketer, I have also been somewhat trained to overcome the discomfort of networking. And of course, if you are starting out, bring along an extrovert friend, let him/her do the heavy lifting for you.

AN INTROVERT NETWORKER WHO WORKS THE ROOM IN STEALTH MODE

Christie Dao is a natural introvert who networks in a stealth mode. She does it so authentically that you don't realise she is "networking".

A Vietnamese, Christie went to America when she was 12. She worked diligently to overcome language and cultural barriers. Determined not to let her college education be a family burden, she charted a plan to get a full scholarship and her eventual dream job back in Asia. Despite being an introvert, Christie thrived in different cultures and built a very diverse network. In fact, she achieved three major career goals through help along the way. Right after graduation, she got her first job in Intel through a career advisor. During her time in Intel, she built an enriching career spanning across two continents, three departments and six functional roles in 16 markets in the Greater Asia region.

Fast forward to 2017, she decided to embark on her coaching certification. Her trainer referred her to an opportunity at Ingeus where I met her. Christie checked out the role and coincidentally, she found that the hiring manager at Ingeus was her ex-colleague. The familiarity did open the door. She got a phone interview with her ex-colleague's manager and the rest was history.

Christie is an unassuming person. The fact that she has held different roles across different cultures and functional roles in more than 20 years is a testament to her good people skills. Her ex-colleague recognised that and at Ingeus, she was assigned to conduct networking workshops. Networking for introverts doesn't come naturally. It is an acquired skill.

Today, Christie is the director, Capability & Organisation Optimisation, at GECO Asia. This role came to her through a network she built at Ingeus. Her blend of IT, sales and marketing experience and coaching helped create a new pathway for her. She is now responsible for growing sales and overseeing the human resource function.

I caught up with Christie and was curious about how she overcame her challenges in networking. This is what she shares:

"I struggle with 'networking' for many years. I tried many different things; some worked and some didn't. One day, I came across two quotes that gave me a confidence booster:

Maya Angelou (poet and storyteller): I've learned that people will forget what you said, people will forget what you did, but people will never forget how you made them feel.

John Q Baucom (author): Don't join a club that doesn't want your membership.

These two quotes guide how I network intentionally.

I realise that I don't have to have 100% success. And I know how to be myself and treat people the way I want to be treated.

I select my events carefully and prepare to talk and add value. I aim to build a relationship with one or two new people per event. Focus on creating value for others. For example, I set aside time to share articles or frameworks that may be of interest to my network."

Her approach towards networking is simple. "Networking is like an emotional bank account. You can only withdraw after you've made a deposit.

"I am reminded of another quote. If you want to go fast, you go alone. If you want to go far, you go together. Networking is a two-way street. It has enriched my life. My network is my networth. Be a relationship-builder!"

SUMMARY

In an increasingly socially-connected world, your network plays an important role in advancing your career – either direct recruitment, job referrals or even giving you knowledge of a new industry. In the future, who you know is what you know. As a recruiter, would you trust a referral from a network or someone who applied for the role based on a job advertisement which may attract more than a few hundred applicants?

When you invest in your network, you are investing in yourself. There are many benefits to building your network. Networking can:

- Contribute to your social well-being.
- Lead to the exchange of ideas and keep you abreast of industry trends.
- Lead to business or job opportunities faster.
- Boost your professional confidence and vouch for your work.
- Lead you to opportunities in very unexpected ways.

These benefits work both ways. When building your network, it is not about "what's in it for me". As Seth Godin, author of *Purple Cow: Transform Your Business by Being Remarkable*, said: "Networking that matters is helping people achieve their goals."

8 TRANS-DISCIPLINARY LEARNING

"In a turbulent world, there's another set of cognitive skills that matters more: the ability to rethink and unlearn."

– *Adam Grant, organisational psychologist and bestselling author*

Over lunch with a 35-year-old colleague, she didn't understand why I was building so many "pathways" – honing my coaching skills, getting myself certified as a human-centred designer and developing many adjacent skills. She had a fairly sheltered career and linear path. Her philosophy was that as we grow older, we should "de-clutter" by living simply and finding peace in what we do. There is no need to create so many paths.

She was not wrong. But when I put on my coaching hat, this felt so limiting. We know that in a volatile world, the ability to learn, relearn and unlearn are assets. Building skills from different domains give you options. You will need to connect the dots and understand what value these skills can bring to organisations or your business. You may even create a career portfolio over time.

For example, I am more left-brain wired – being academically trained in economics and statistics. But as I progress in my career, I tapped on my right brain – uncovering consumer insights, understanding user psychology, and developing creative campaigns to influence consumer behaviour. By now being trained in two different domains has helped me professionally. My role now requires me to be a master of data and voice of the customer. Besides building depth, I can now connect the dots and understand the wider implication of my job.

Let me share a story. There was a hit movie *Babe* (1995) starring James Cromwell and Babe, the pig. (It was even nominated for Best Picture at the Oscars that year!)

In the movie, Babe, the lovable star, is brought to the farm and innocently roams freely until one day, he realised to his horror what pigs on a farm end up as... bacon! Terrified, he realised that if he continued 'just being a pig', his fate would be no different from the hundreds of his piggy pals and presumably be placed on people's platters.

He started looking around the farm and observed the other animals. Then an idea came to him that could potentially save his life. He decided to take on the job of a sheepdog (or 'sheep pig', as he insisted on being called). He became so good at his new role that Farmer Hoggett enrolled him in a sheepdog competition where he won the grand prize... and was spared from becoming smoked ham.

He literally reinvented himself by building new skills – shepherding the sheep! There is a big lesson here. Because in today's VUCA world, we need to be like Babe, constantly reinventing ourselves to avoid being disrupted involuntarily. Or for that matter, be willing to reinvent even if you are disrupted.

I wrote about importance of learning agility in Chapter 2. While it is important to be a lifelong learner, you need to be strategic in planning your learning roadmap otherwise it will create confusion. Know what you are really good at and find ways to deepen this circle of competence. Then identify the skills in the periphery of this circle that will enhance what you are already doing. For example, recently I attended a talent management programme conducted by the Korn Ferry Academy. Although it is meant for human resource practitioners, I found it incredibly useful in shaping my thinking as a functional manager.

The programme has equipped me with the knowledge on talent development, talent engagement and the different talent competency frameworks. In my opinion, if you are in a senior management role, these are important knowledge for you to maximise your impact as a leader.

There are four approaches you can take in your learning:

1. Upskill

We have first-hand experienced how fast technology has changed the way we work and live just over a period of two years. As a result, organisations had to accelerate their transformation to keep up with the change in consumer behaviour. For instance, with a huge drop in travel during the pandemic, Airbnb started to help hosts financially and connect them with potential guests. The hosts can now offer online events focused on cooking, meditation, art therapy, magic, songwriting, virtual tours and other activities, with users joining for a modest fee. Many roles had also evolved as technology continues taking over the more routine work. Therefore we have to keep upgrading our skill set. Just like how we upgrade our wardrobe every year to keep up with fashion trends.

2. Cross-skill

Learning skills from domains other than your current core competency to perform beyond existing responsibilities is termed as cross-skilling or cross-training. For example, a marketer needs to cross-skill and understand technology platforms because technology will enable tracking of performance campaigns. In the same way, a marketer needs to be competent in both data analysis and human psychology to draw out insights that will help develop the right messaging to customers.

Cross-skilling also helps employees gain a better understanding of the process from start to finish. This boosts job satisfaction as well.

3. Deep skill

While cross-skilling is spreading one's skill set breadth-wise, expert skilling is going in deep. These are the skills that help you go deeper in your profession, deeper in your leadership, deeper in establishing your personal brand. For example, a doctor may choose to specialise in a particular field such as neurosurgery. So, to deepen his skills, he will continually upgrade his knowledge of technology to help in neurosurgery.

4. Reskill

Reskilling involves training on an entirely new set of skills to prepare you to take on a different role within the company. This typically occurs when your previous tasks or responsibilities become irrelevant, often due to advances in technology. This would also apply if you wish to do a mid-career switch because your previous roles no longer exist in the industry.

The rise of hybrid careers

Millions of jobs will be created or destroyed by technological disruption over the next decade. Yet the most profound and unnoticed trend in today's labour market is how technology is mutating jobs into new, unexpected hybrid jobs.

In a research by GetSmarter, an online learning platform, it found that a candidate who has strong hybrid skills would have a mix of both the hard and soft skills relevant for the new economy. In fact, there is a rising trend of a hybrid professional. These roles are resistant to automation and in high demand. For example, possessing a combination of skills such as marketing and statistical analysis or design and programming is fast becoming a prerequisite.

Hybrid jobs have several qualities that set them apart from other jobs. While these jobs may be technological- and data-driven, they also require human qualities like making judgement and creativity. Hybrid jobs rarely involve rote and repetitive tasks. Because of this, they are more likely to demand a combination of skills like critical thinking, leadership, problem solving and collaboration.

According to Burning Glass Institute, here's a look at some of the hybrid roles and how these roles can boost your salary:

- Marketing managers received an average salary of US$71,000, but when they possessed database management competency in SQL, their average salary was US$100,000, a premium of 41%.

- Civil engineers were paid an average of US$78,000 but when strong people-management skills were added to the mix, their compensation rose to US$87,000, a 12% premium.

- Project managers received an average salary of US$75,000, but when they were skilled in Tableau, a visual analytics platform transforming the way we use data to solve problems, they boosted their pay to US$85,000, a 13% premium.

- General managers earned an average salary of US$63,000, but those managers with strong data analysis skills secured an average salary of US$81,000, a 29% premium.

- Customer service managers were paid an average salary of US$49,000, but managers with expertise in Customer Relationship Management or CRM earned an average of US$60,000, a premium of 22%.

In Chapter 2, I mentioned building a career lattice. Besides your functional skills and knowledge, these are nine competencies you need to stay ahead as organisations embark on their digital transformation

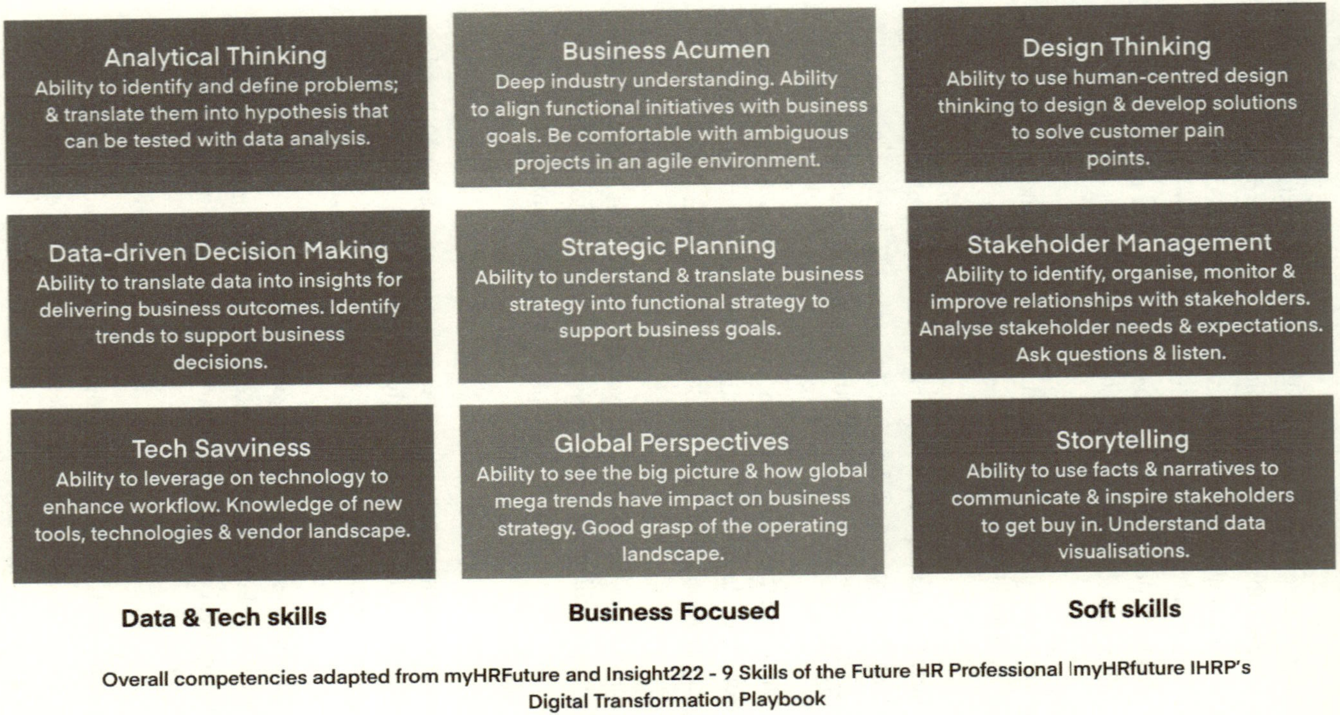

FIGURE 8.1. *Multi-disciplinary learning and nine essential skills for the future of work.*

journey. As a marketer, performing well in my domain area is not sufficient. I also have to be comfortable with data and technology, have a good business sense and understanding of the operating environment. Softer skills are also important in a more connected world.

FIGURE 8.1 lists the nine competencies that's important for the future of work. See if you can tick off the list. You need not achieve top scores for each competency. But, be aware of what you are lacking and what you are good at so that you can either develop them or focus on work that leverages more on your strengths.

Develop integrative thinking

Complexity is not going away in the future of work. We will encounter many diverse perspectives as we work with multiple generations and people across borders. When taking a trans-disciplinary approach to learning, you may even have very opposing views or ideas. How do you deal with such tensions of opposing ideas? Author Roger Martin of *A New Way to Think* defines this new way of thinking as integrative thinking. He explains it as "the ability to face constructively the tension of opposing ideas and, instead of choosing one at the expense of the other, generate a creative resolution of the tension in the form of a new idea that contains elements of the opposing ideas but is superior to each".

In the future of work, you will need to move from conventional thinking to integrative thinking. Here's an illustration of the difference:

Convention thinking = We can build either a low-cost, low-quality yacht, or a high-cost, high-quality yacht.

Integrative thinking = Maybe we are not limited to one option or the other. What are some of our other ideas? How can we build an affordable and yet high-quality yacht?

This form of thinking helps us uncover creative solutions that we might have overlooked. This is an important skill to help organisations innovate. The top skill outlook by World Economic Forum is analytical thinking and innovation. Therefore, developing integrative thinking will position you well for the future.

Work skills in the past were mainly separated and distinct or siloed. The future of work, by contrast, draws on skill sets from diverging fields. For example, marketing will increasingly require a combination of creative thinking with data analysis – requiring marketing managers to be designers and analysts rolled into one. In computer science, once considered highly technical work, software developers require communications skills, problem-solving skills, creative and research skills, and skills in teamwork and collaboration.

Do a regular audit

While you are on the drive to gain knowledge, remember to do a regular audit of market needs and the competitive landscape to check that you are building skills that the market needs.

In businesses, authors of *Blue Ocean Strategy* Renée Mauborgne and W Chan Kim coined the terms 'red' and 'blue' oceans to denote the market universe. Red oceans are all the industries in existence today – the known marketspace, where industry boundaries are defined and companies try to outperform their rivals to grab a greater share of the existing market. Cutthroat competition turns the ocean blood red. Hence, the term 'red' oceans. Blue oceans, on the other hand, denote all the industries not in existence today – the unknown marketspace, unexplored and untainted by competition. Like the 'blue' ocean, it is vast, deep and powerful – in terms of opportunity and profitable growth.

This is a good analogy for how you should navigate your learning journey and career. When there are too many like you vying for the same role, you are competing in the red ocean. Do an audit of your unique skill, uncover how your hybrid knowledge or experience can serve an opportunity. Don't look for jobs, look for problems you can solve and pitch it to the prospective employer or business. And potentially create a new role for yourself. That is the blue ocean.

A HYBRID PROFESSIONAL WITH LEARNING AGILITY

I met Sam Li only recently when he became a fellow mentor at MentorsHub – a social initiative to mentor young adults to improve their social mobility. Prior to this, he was a mentee in 2015.

Over dinner, I got to hear about his interesting career – a data scientist with a business background, and how he proactively charts his career and takes a trans-disciplinary approach to learning.

A graduate in electrical engineering, his passion for technology led him to pursue a PhD in research specialising in "smart grid", which includes Internet of Things (IoT), artificial intelligence (AI), machine learning, data science, blockchain and statistics. Naturally his earlier career was in research engineering and data science at A*STAR (Agency for Science, Technology and Research) and Hewlett-Packard respectively. His current career at Dell saw him start as a principal data scientist, leading a team of data scientists before becoming a global product business leader (involving AI and data science). He is currently pursuing his Master of Business Administration at Imperial College London.

I posed a few questions to him:

What is your approach to navigating your career?
I have always taken time every year to review my career. I try to understand what I have done in the past year and write the key highlights for that year. In addition, I will frequently research online for different job roles for my next career move, especially on LinkedIn, where I explore people with similar careers in my current position and look at their next move.

Of course, there is no exact similar career for everyone. However, I will reflect on what I lack and the gaps required to develop my next role. Most of my career moves are not conventional, but the more different it gets, the more exposure and learning curve that needs to be built. I make it an effort to build knowledge and skills from different domains. On hindsight, it is very useful as it gives me richer perspectives and helps me make better decisions at work.

What motivated you to take on a business role?

The triggering point was when I was appointed to cover the data science manager role in the team for Hewlett Packard Enterprise. During my first role as a people manager, I encountered a lot of difficulty handling a data science team.

We needed to combine the business and science domains to deliver business objectives for the organisation. The problems made me realise my lack of understanding of business theories.

This made strategising for the team a key challenge in the long-term.

The experience motivated me to pursue a business degree. I realised that most key decision stakeholders have business-centric mindsets, which is complex for technologists to comprehend. Therefore, I wanted to bridge the gaps through a technologist business role to make up the difference and be the catalyst to improve corporate coherence for the team.

Data/technology (left-brained) vs business (more right-brained) – which is your passion?

My true passion is still in data/technology at this career phase. However, business is one of the key domains that will enable the progress of data/technology. Hence, I am looking forward to building my career in technology management or technology strategist/consultancy roles.

How has this trans-disciplinary approach in learning helped you in your thinking/work?

The trans-disciplinary approach expands my perspectives, allowing me to understand other jobs' requirements and problems. In addition, it helps me see the bigger picture within the industry and understand the impact of emerging technology trends on business.

The trans-disciplinary approach primarily improves my communications with diverse functional groups. It was an eye-opener because I was only speaking to technologists in the past, which narrowed my point of view in the working world.

How do you see the future of work? How should employees keep themselves relevant?
My view on the future of work will always be to look at the emerging trend and adapt to it. As the world keeps improving and changing for every generation, people should be adaptive in order to build a better future.

Employees can keep themselves relevant if they recognise the industry shifts, understand their key capabilities, and put in the effort to adjust with an open mind. Instilling a growth mindset is the key to relevancy in the workforce.

SUMMARY

Building skills from a different domain gives you more career options. The emergence of new technology will see more industries converging and many roles will evolve. There will be a greater demand for people with the dexterity to handle jobs that require both left- and right-brain functions, giving rise to hybrid careers.

When the turbulent period caused by Covid-19 took us by surprise, many of us found ourselves unprepared for new roles. Legendary investor Warren Buffet said, "Only when the tide goes out do you discover who's been swimming naked". The message here is don't wait for the storm to hit, reinvent and get ahead of it.

Stay open to new knowledge and watch the trends to upskill, cross-skill and deep skill. Increasingly, we will see companies hire for learnability and train for skill.

The future of work belongs to those who are always curious and have the learning agility.

CREATE THE FUTURE YOU

The oldest client that I have coached is a 72-year-old man. When I first saw him, he was well-groomed, with hair combed neatly, wearing a white long-sleeved shirt and tight fitting pants. This was in 2017.

He came to me for coaching as his employment contract with an educational institution as a procurement director ended three years ago when he was 69 years. (In Singapore, the official retirement age then was 62 years and the employer had the right to renew the contract annually based on new employment terms.)

He was healthy and had all the time on his hands and felt bored. He was also not keen to look after his grandchildren and was not in need of the money as his house was all paid up. But he was keen to get back to employment. I explored a few options with him. For example, join a non-profit organisation to offer his experience to review cost structure and procurement practices, become a volunteer at a non-profit organisation such as providing tuition to low-income families or be a befriender to the disabled/seniors, or even start his own online retail business. But he insisted that he would only work in an office environment and if he got paid.

A few weeks later, he wrote to me that he was feeling depressed as he couldn't find any roles that suited him. I suggested he could lend his experience and work for free in charities and leverage his network to get back to paid jobs as a consultant. Surely the non-profit organisations would need help in managing their vendor and procurement processes to save costs. Besides charity work would be good for his mental well-being. After that suggestion, I never heard from him.

Did his work identity become his own identity that he couldn't think of what else to do besides his professional experience of procurement? In a world where work constitutes a big part of our lives, it is no wonder our identity is so closely linked to our work. How do you feel when you are asked to think about your future? You would have been so used to thinking about the three stages of life – study, work and retire. The average mortality age in the world is 71 years old. While an average Singaporean can live up to 83 years old. What would you do after the official retirement age of 63 years old in Singapore (as of 1st July 2022). For people like my client who failed to think ahead and reinvent himself, he just continued working as long as he could. His job was his purpose. In this case, he could have reinvented himself to be a consultant or advisor to a non-profit organisation.

While this book has been focusing on reinventing yourself to thrive in your career, we must not forget that career is only one part in the larger scheme of things. In fact, Brian Dyson, president and CEO of Coca-Cola, had a different perspective. He shared during his speech at the Georgia Tech 172nd commencement address in 1996 that we have to juggle five balls in our life – work, family, health, friends and spirit.

Work is a rubber ball. If you drop it, it will bounce back. But the other four balls – family, health, friends and spirit – are made of glass. If you drop one of these, they will be irrevocably scuffed, marked, nicked, damaged or even shattered. They will never be the same. You must understand that and prioritise accordingly. "Value has a value only if it is valued," said Dyson.

As we go through different decades in our lives, we need to recalibrate, refresh and reinvent ourselves. Studies have shown that many people experienced a cliff drop after retirement (from a corporate role) particularly if they have over-identified with their careers (FIGURE 9.1).

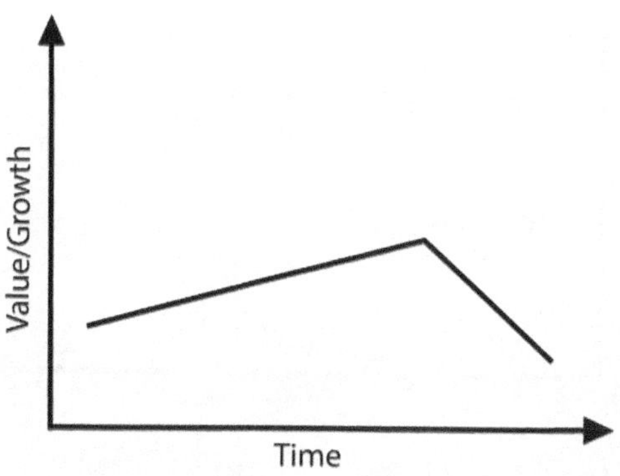

FIGURE 9.1. *The linear life.*

In our lifetime, at different life stages, our northstar or purpose will evolve. Our priorities may change or we may experience something that pushes us in a different direction. We may also reach the goal that we set for ourselves, which means it's time to set a new target. This could mean an extension of our current goal or a new one altogether. Therefore it is good that you review your northstar regularly to chart your next trajectory.

In FIGURE 9.2, it shows that our lives will comprise of many cycles. It is up to us to reinvent ourselves to build our next trajectory where success is not measured on material wealth but by the purposeful life we lead.

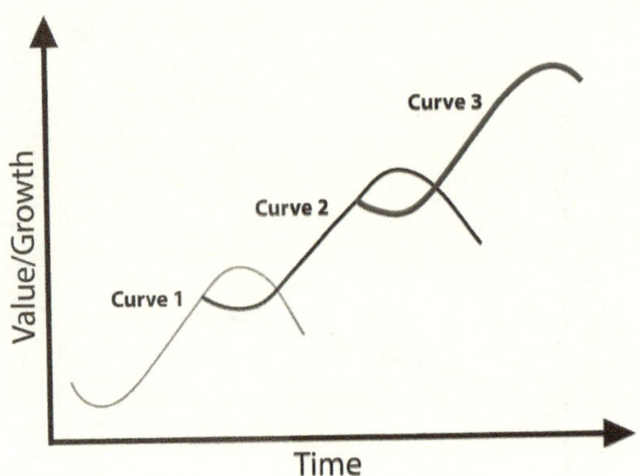

FIGURE 9.2. *The cyclical life of constant reinvention.*

Letting go and taking stock

Reinventing yourself doesn't have to be throwing away the old and doing something entirely different. It doesn't mean you reinvent yourself from being a musician to a data scientist, or from a corporate executive to an entrepreneur. You could if you wish to do so.

It could simply be a shift in your mindset or mental model. Letting go here could be giving up something that hasn't worked for you. You could ask – ***"Is there anything in my life that I am doing today that, knowing what I now know, I wouldn't get into again today if I had to do it over again?"*** This is a great thinking tool – zero-based thinking. For example, while I enjoy coaching, I do not like the monotony of paperwork involved in a coaching role in a government agency. Having an awareness of what I do not enjoy helps me simplify my thinking and eliminate options.

You would also need to reflect on your past and find your leverage when you reinvent. Three key questions you need to reflect on are:

1. What are your non-negotiable values?

Your values create boundaries and benchmarks for big decisions. They distil the possibilities of what to pursue, and they help to determine the next steps. Making decisions aligned to your values and belief system feels affirming and satisfying, even when those choices may be difficult.

Questions to ask yourself:
- What are the top values that are non-negotiable?
- What would you have done differently in your life?
- What are you most proud of?
- Are there areas in your life where you feel out of balance or that you are missing something?

Like what Adam Grant, author of *Think Again: The Power of Knowing What You Don't Know*, says, "Big career decisions don't come with a map, but all you need is a compass. In an unpredictable world, you can't make a master plan. You can only gauge whether you're on a meaningful path. The right next move is the one that brings you a step closer to living your core values".

2. What drives you?

Drivers are personal motivators and intrinsic. It is what gets you excited and energised. For example, to some people, accomplishments, sense of belonging, creativity or solving problems drives them. To some, being able to make a positive impact in the community or specifically in climate change fires them up. A deep reflection on what motivates you internally would help you connect the dots forward.

3. What are your strengths?

The Pareto Principle, also known as the 80/20 rule, states that 80% of consequences come from 20% of the causes. What this means is leverage on your natural talent and professional competencies to create the future you.

I use Gallup Clifton StrengthsFinder to uncover my own talents. It is an assessment used by more than 2.3 million people globally. It comprises of 34 talent themes across four leadership domains such as executing, influencing, relationship building and strategic thinking.

Talents, Clifton writes, are your "naturally recurring patterns of thought, feeling or behaviour. They're the innate, natural abilities you can productively apply". To turn those talents into strengths, you must invest in them – practise using them and adding knowledge and skills to them.

I have found the Gallup Strengths very useful as I connect the dots backward. I naturally gravitate towards roles that best leverage on my talents. Having this knowledge also helps me identify the type of work that best suits me. If you want to find out your strengths, here's the link to the test –www.gallup.com/cliftonstrengths/en/253850/cliftonstrengths-for-individuals.aspx. The test comes with a full report.

In addition, you can leverage on your professional competency and strong professional network to build your next trajectory of success.

Reflecting on your past can help you recalibrate your future. But it will not be transformational.

Playing the long game

Stephen Covey writes in his book *The 7 Habits of Highly Effective People* about the habit of "Begin with the end in mind". Here's some questions that may get you started:

- Who do I want to become?

- What is my new northstar? (purpose)
- What would make me happy?
- What's my mission statement? (a mission statement articulates who you want to be and do. Why you do what you do and who do you serve? It is your plan for success, one that puts your goals in focus and moves your ideas to reality.)

To do this, you need some imagination or visualisation. Your vision is the magnetic force that pushes you to achieve your dreams or aspirations.

In 1996, Professor Judd Blaslotto of the University of Chicago took three groups of students to test each group on how many points they scored with a limited number of throws to test the power of visualisation. In the lead up to the test:

Group 1 was instructed not to touch a basketball.
Group 2 was instructed to visualise free throws for one hour every day.
Group 3 simply visualised making free throws.

After 30 days, Blaslotto tested them again:

Group 1 showed no improvement.
Group 2 showed a 24% improvement.
Group 3 showed a 23% improvement.

When you visualise what your future is going to look like and also take stock of your past, you are able to work on the gaps to create the future you.

I often ask my clients "What would an 80-year-old 'YOU' thank you for what you do today?" This is a reflective question that puts them in a state of gratitude. It often elicits an answer that surprises the clients themselves.

Keeping your life in balance

With a longer lifespan, a person who is 50 years old today is only halfway through his/her productive work life. You have more time than you think. There is more reason than ever to continually re-evaluate, recalibrate and reinvent at different phases of life.

You may be at a crossroads, wondering which way to turn and what the best path is or transiting to a new season or phase of life and wanting to make the most of it. Or you could be excited about a new role that's coming up and ready to chart a new trajectory. Or you are simply enjoying where your life is right now and wanting to live it fully. Regardless of where you are now, you need to continuously move and not rest on your laurels, yet at the same time, keep a balance while you move. The key to keeping your life in balance is to set your peace of mind and spirituality, your happiness, and your home life as your anchors and organise your life around them. When you are able to keep this in balance, you will live a more fulfilling life as you continue to reinvent yourself.

Here's a Wheel of Life (FIGURE 9.3) with different parts of your life. You can use it to check on your balance. This is a useful tool when life gets out of balance, such as suffering from workaholism, getting burned out, or generally being unsatisfied and not sure why.

In each dimension, rate how satisfied you are at the present moment on a scale of one to 10, with 10 being the most satisfied. Once done, compare the ratings across the dimensions. Some will undoubtedly be higher than others. The question is – are you happy with the trade-offs? Something has to give and sometimes it is ok to achieve a lower score on some dimensions as that may not be a priority. For example, if you are a new parent, you may be scoring low on "friendship" and that may not be so important to you at this time. Or if you are retiring, career might no longer be important to you, but you could reinvent to work in a different capacity such as taking on board seats or providing consultancy work that can still leverage on your expertise and not letting your experience go to waste.

The success metrics for each dimension is for you to define. What's important is you are happy with the overall balance and trade-offs.

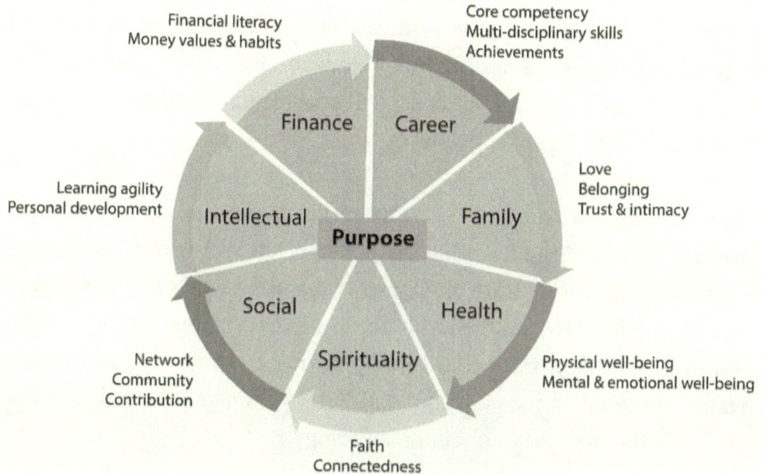

FIGURE 9.3. *The Wheel of Life that will keep you in balance as you REINVENT yourself.*

If you want to put this into practice, you can download the resources from my website at reinvent.adelinetiah.com.

Life will be a series of reinventions as you redefine what the new success looks like.

The story of Kodak and Fujifilm

Let me share a story of Fujifilm to illustrate the importance of constant reinvention.

During the 1970s, the photography business was badly impacted when the price of silver jumped tenfold, from US$5 to US$50 per ounce. Silver was an essential ingredient in photo processing and manufacturers like Kodak and Fujifilm were concerned about business failures. Fortunately, when the price plummeted again in 1980, Kodak and the other photography businesses settled back to business as usual. And they soon forgot about the earlier crisis. Fujifilm's new CEO Minoru Ohnishi however had a very different mindset. He was determined to reinvent and prepare the organisation for a radical shift in the photography business. Once Sony introduced its digital camera in 1984, he started building diverse digital capabilities.

By 2003, Fujifilm had over 4,000 mini digital processing labs in chain stores throughout the US while Kodak had fewer than 100. Soon they began experimenting with their own capabilities. Fujifilm discovered that some ingredients of the film could be used in the field of beauty. The four basic film-related technologies that Fujifilm used to develop beauty products were collagen research, light analysis and control, antioxidation, and original nanotechnology.

"We put a very strong antioxidation ingredient into our photographic products in order to stop the colour from fading as time goes by and we decided to do this for our skincare products too," said Shigetaka Komori, the former CEO, Fujifilm.

So in 2007, Fujifilm boldly launched a high-end skincare range called ASTALIFT. With a subtle reference to its origins, ASTALIFT aimed to deliver "photogenic beauty" to its customers.

Long before Kodak filed for bankruptcy in 2012, Fujifilm was enjoying diversified annual revenues of over US$20 billion with only a minor contribution coming from its photographic products. By 2020, Fujifilm reported revenues of US$22.1 billion, with global healthcare including cosmetics contributing 22% or US$4.9 billion to that sum. That was a stellar showcase of reinvention, building new revenue streams in

beauty and even in healthcare, while maintaining its digital photography business.

Technology doesn't get to decide the future, you do

The story above shows that we cannot be complacent like Kodak or like the frog in slow boiling water. Technology, geopolitical tensions and many black swan events will continue to disrupt our lives. We need to embrace the mindset of constant reinvention. To ensure that your life stays on the trajectory of increasing success (as defined by you), your goal is to become a master of change rather than a victim of change.

The eight traits in the REINVENT framework are timeless and practical. Whether you are in a mid-career rut, planning a new career path or mulling over what's next, I hope this book will give you a new lens to look at the future. Every inflection point in the future is an opportunity to reinvent yourself.

If 2020 to 2022 were years of unplanned reinvention because of unexpected disruptions, then 2023 is when it gets intentional because we all know that changes are happening at a staggering speed.

Are you ready to ride the waves of transformation?

REDEFINING SUCCESS WITH A NEW PURPOSE

I met Candice Goh at Halftime Summit in 2013. The Halftime Summit is run by Halftime Asia to facilitate reflection of one's success and accomplishments so to discover one's purpose for the next stage of life.

Candice is such an unassuming and carefree person; you wouldn't imagine that she was once a managing director of global consulting company Accenture. She spent more than 20 years climbing the corporate ladder and spending days solving client problems and reaping profits for the companies. Across more than 10 countries that she worked in, there was one common theme. People worked hard to make a living, to have a better life, to provide for their families, and to satisfy their material wants – bigger paychecks, bigger cars, bigger houses, etc. The world defines success by material achievements.

A series of illnesses from 2009 to 2011 was a wake-up call for Candice. After achieving success in her career, what's next? How much is enough? She was searching for something bigger and finding a bigger purpose in life. The Halftime Summit was pivotal in her journey and search for significance.

Since she was 15, Candice wanted to make a difference. The Halftime Summit revisited this question – how do you want to be remembered?

At 44 years old, she decided to reinvent herself. Getting off the corporate treadmill was bittersweet. But she found her northstar – to empower others to maximise their true potential. She builds a new identity as a breakthrough coach, a role that is aligned with her values and strengths. Leveraging her corporate experiences, she also provides strategic consulting as part of her professional services. And in 2021, she was conferred a honorary doctorate, fulfilling her dream to be Dr Candice Goh.

Today, she is living her best life and enjoying purposeful freedom. We are all familiar with the terms "financial freedom" and "time freedom" – having the money and time to do whatever we desire. "Purposeful freedom" brings this a notch higher to align our finances and time towards contributing to a purpose that benefits others.

Aligning to her purposeful freedom, Candice is the co-founder of MentorsHub, a social mentorship initiative with a passion in enhancing the capabilities and opportunities of young adults. She is also the author of two self-help books – *From Piece to Peace* and *Rise Above You*. As a breakthrough coach, she has helped many clients achieve personal and corporate breakthroughs.

Candice is able to achieve the freedom today because she started her financial planning when she was in her early 30s. Today, her books and her work are all focused on inspiring people to pursue their dreams, to go from good to great and from success to significance.

Quoting one of her clients Luke Ong, "Candice changed the trajectory of my life!"

Candice is truly a person who walks the talk. She is a living example of someone who is courageous enough to take action and steer her life towards purposeful freedom.

When I asked her what advice she could give to people to create their future, Candice shares:

"I think most people will hold on to job security, especially if they're at a senior level and drawing a high salary. The opportunity costs could seem too high. The book by Bronnie Ware called *The Top Five Regrets of the Dying* has made me realise how important it is for us to live a life true to ourselves as we really don't know when we'll expire.

Living a purposeful and meaningful life could mean different things to different people. I know of many people who find meaning in their jobs. But if you're someone who hates your job, then I'll really encourage you to re-examine your options. It's your life, make it count for yourself."

Candice is constantly learning and upgrading herself. One of her favourite quotes by theoretical physicist Albert Einstein: "The day you stop learning, you start dying".

Even as she helps her clients to achieve their breakthroughs, she is also constantly achieving her own breakthroughs. She has inspired me to achieve my own breakthrough too, by writing this book.

SUMMARY

We spend a large part of our lives in our jobs and to some, build a career. It is natural that we have built our identity around our work without realising it. For some, it takes a major illness to bring clarity on what is important for them, who they want to become and what they want to do. For many, they just go with the flow and live out the three stages of life – education, then work and finally retirement.

If we expect to live to be 100, it will mean our work lives will stretch over 60 years! As our economy is transforming fast, new jobs will be created, many companies will die, sectors will change, new technologies will require new skills and the way we work will undergo further changes. Who could possibly plan for a 60-year career in a fast-changing environment? The only certainty is that constant reinvention is necessary to avoid complete boredom and to get new skills when the old ones become obsolete.

In our lifetime, we will need to create many Sigmoid curves as we seek to live a life of purpose. In this concluding chapter, there are three key steps you need to take to write your future:

1. **Letting go and taking stock**
   - Understand your strengths, values and drivers to help you calibrate your next step.
   - Harness insights from what has worked or failed as you build your next trajectory.

2. **Playing the long game**
   - Think in decades and visualise who you want to become.
   - Find your purpose and align your actions today to your long-term goals.

3. Keeping in balance

- Your career is not your life. Don't over-index it even when you are having a whale of a time at work.
- Find your balance across the Wheel of Life at different life stages.

With this new lens, life stages will become age-agnostic. Invest in your new trajectory while you are still growing, just like Fujifilm. Keep reinventing!

EPILOGUE

Being an author has always been my childhood dream. So I finally did it.

It has been an amazing learning journey for me. It took all of nine months for the book to be finally published.

The idea of writing a book was a goal I set in 2020 (pre-Covid-19). A coaching session in late 2021 ignited my energy again. After two years of the pandemic, work from home protocol and an accelerated changing landscape, I felt that I had to prioritise achieving my goals over achieving business goals. So my writing journey started officially in February 2022.

Writing this has been cathartic. It was a reflective process of my past achievements and missteps. It has also pushed me out of my comfort zone to look to the future, talk to many thought leaders, read up on the Fourth Industrial Revolution, and how it is impacting our work and lives. I spent my time devouring literature on organisational culture, best practices and learning about Web 3.0 and how these are going to have a great impact on how we work and live.

In writing this, I have learned so much about myself – my agility and capacity to write a book and my willingness to take risks. It was a tough journey as I wanted to give up several times. Thankfully I have a community of writers, and a dedicated publisher and editor who kept pushing the boundaries and encouraging me on this journey.

And I am not really done with writing. I have written two bonus chapters – *A look into the future* and *How I reinvented myself working for a startup*. These chapters are a continuation of where I left off in this book. They can be downloaded from reinvent.adelinetiah.com.

I am glad I finally took time out to share my leadership experiences – my successes and failures, and insights from my coaching experiences. I enjoy having business conversations at work with leaders. And I love having people development conversations with people under my charge. These experiences have given me stories to share.

Experiences like these make us human and become critical building blocks of our growth. Our lives and most exhilarating memories are defined by our courageous act to reinvent – the times when the odds were not in our favour but we nonetheless prevail.

By now, I hope you will have a fresh set of lens through which to perceive disruption. And you would be inspired to embrace a mindset of constant reinvention.

As I finish writing this book, I am more optimistic than ever about the possibilities and new opportunities in the Fourth Industrial Revolution.

What's next?

I have shared many stories and lessons learnt. It's now your turn to craft your story and be in the driver seat of your career and future.

To help you move forward, I would like to invite you to download free tools and resources from reinvent.adelinetiah.com by simply scanning the QR code below.

Do connect with me on www.linkedin.com/in/adeline-tiah and I would love to hear from you on your own journey of reinvention.

ACKNOWLEDGEMENTS

As the saying goes "it takes a village to raise a child"; this is a very apt analogy for producing this book. Although I hold the pen, this book would not have been completed without a team of people behind me.

The first content idea was sparked over a coaching conversation with my coach Adam Turner at Standard Chartered Bank. I was "oscillating", work wasn't quite exciting and I kept thinking about the opportunity cost of staying where I was. I felt like a hamster running around a wheel in a cage – going nowhere. I thought, if I wasn't going to write a book, when would it ever happen? I decided to take time off from the corporate ladder. Over six months, after five iterations and 20 revisions, this book is finally produced.

Firstly, I like to thank Charlie Ang for his insights on the future of work. Your thought leadership and generous sharing have helped me develop depth in my writing. And special thanks to Dr Candice Goh who not only pushed me to get started but was also my book critic. You offered a very different perspective and helped me sharpen my thinking.

Special thanks to the brilliant people who provided feedback as I wrote the book – Christie Dao, Christina Lim, Jennifer Tan, Melody Wong and Elena Chow. Many thanks to my interviewees who gave their time for the book: Sophia Yeow, Elena Chow, Ean Yeo, Eugene Seah, Eric

Sim, Chin Sau Yong, Christie Dao, Dr Sam Li and Dr Candice Goh. Your stories and wisdom are truly inspiring. And there are many more whose paths I have crossed in the last six months, who were so open to give me feedback on the book theme, title and book cover. Thank you; every bit of feedback counts.

And thank you to my publisher Phoon Kok Hwa of Candid Creation Publishing for setting a high bar and for taking a punt on me. Eleanor Yap's rigorous editorial review and always encouraging me on this journey. Thank you both for your patience and generous advice.

Last but not least, to my husband Calvin and my son Daniel for your unconditional love and silent support; giving me the space and focus to complete this book.

And most important of all, none of this would be possible without God who constantly reminds me *"those who wait on the Lord shall renew their strength. They shall mount up with wings like eagles, they shall run and not be weary, they shall walk and not faint" (Isaiah 40:31 NKJV).* This gives me the strength and courage to take time out to share my experience and insights. I hope this in turn gives you, my readers the strength and courage to reinvent yourself and thrive in the uncertainty ahead.

ABOUT THE AUTHOR

ADELINE T H TIAH is an accomplished marketer with more than 20 years' experience across top banks, telco and startups. She is passionate about building brands and high-performance teams. A certified practitioner in human-centred design thinking, Adeline facilitates design thinking workshops at work and in universities. She is currently an adjunct lecturer at a Singapore university, teaching a module on digital and social media marketing. Adeline also partners with organisations to help them identify strategic blind spots, create their value propositions and develop their go-to-market strategies. A keynote speaker in marketing and leadership forums, Adeline's mission is to help organisations build their businesses and transform lives.

Adeline is also an International Coaching Federation-certified executive coach with more than 250 hours of coaching experience. With her reinvent mindset, she stays abreast of emerging trends to find opportunities for growth, and build her network and multi-disciplinary skills. She constantly renews and reinvents to stay agile and antifragile in the face of disruptions.

BIBLIOGRAPHY

Bommel, Dr Tara Van. "The Power of Empathy in Times of Crisis and Beyond." https://www.catalyst.org/reports/empathy-work-strategy-crisis/?utm_medium=web&utm_source=release&utm_campaign=IWD22&utm_content=3122. Accessed 1 July 2022.

CareerBuilder. https://www.prnewswire.com/news-releases/more-than-half-of-employers-have-found-content-on-social-media-that-caused-them-not-to-hire-a-candidate-according-to-recent-careerbuilder-survey-300694437.html. Accessed 23 May 2022.

CB Insights. "Banking is only the beginning: 65 big industries blockchain could transform." https://www.cbinsights.com/research/industries-disrupted-blockchain. Accessed 14 August 2022.

Clark, Dorie. *The Long Game: How to Be a Long-Term Thinker in a Short-Term World.* Harvard Business Review Press, 2021.

Dimock, Michael. "Defining generations: Where Millennials end and Generation Z begins." https://www.pewresearch.org/fact-tank/2019/01/17/where-millennials-end-and-generation-z-begins/. Accessed 30 April 2022.

Epstein, David. *Range: Why Generalists Triumph in a Specialized World.* Riverhead Books, 2019.

Finch, Caleb. "History of Companies and Industries Listed on the S&P 500." https://www.qad.com/blog/2019/10/sp-500-companies-over-time. Accessed 15 April 2022.

GetSmarter. "The future of work is here." https://www.getsmarter.com/blog/future-of-work/. Accessed 30 June 2022.

Goldsmith, Marshall and Reiter, Mark. *The Earned Life: Lose Regret, Choose Fulfilment.* Currency, 2022.

Granovetter, Mark S. "The Strength of Weak Ties." American Journal of Sociology 78, no 6 (1973): 1371.

Grant, Adam. *Think Again: The Power of Knowing What You Don't Know.* Viking Publishing, 2021.

Gratton, Lynda and Scott, Andrew J. *The 100-Year Life: Living and Working in an Age of Longevity.* Bloomsbury Information, 2016.

Hayes, Dr Adam. "Blockchain Facts: What Is It, How It Works, and How It Can Be Used." https://www.investopedia.com/terms/b/blockchain.asp. Accessed 1 August 2022.

Hoffman, Reid and Casnocha, Ben. *The Startup of You: Adapt, Take Risks, Grow Your Network, and Transform Your Career.* Currency, 2012.

Hunt, Dame Vivian, Layton, Dennis and Prince, Sara. "Why diversity matters." https://www.mckinsey.com/capabilities/people-and-organizational-performance/our-insights/why-diversity-matters. Accessed 23 August 2022.

Kim, Paul. "Understanding web3: The new version of the web that works on blockchain." https://www.businessinsider.com/personal-finance/what-is-web3. Accessed 1 August 2022.

Malhotra, Hem. "What Is The True Effect Of Blockchain On Modern Businesses?" https://www.forbes.com/sites/sap/2022/03/31/what-is-the-true-effect-of-blockchain-on-modern-businesses/?sh=cc4e103b83f5. Accessed 1 August 2022.

Marr, Bernard. *Business Trends in Practice: The 25+ Trends That are Redefining Organizations.* Wiley Publishing, 2021.

McCullen, Aidan. *Undisruptable: A Mindset of Permanent Reinvention for Individuals, Organisations and Life.* Wiley Publishing, 2021.

Qualtrics. "The other COVID-19 crisis: Mental health." https://www.qualtrics.com/blog/confronting-mental-health/. Accessed 15 May 2022.

Taleb, Nassim Nicholas. *Antifragile: Things That Gain from Disorder.* Random House, 2012.